TEACHER'S PET PUBLICATIONS

LITPLAN TEACHER PACK
for

Jacob Have I Loved
based on the book by
Katherine Paterson

Written by
Janine H. Sherman

© 1996 Teacher's Pet Publications
All Rights Reserved

This **LitPlan** for Katherine Patterson's
Jacob Have I Loved
has been brought to you by Teacher's Pet Publications, Inc.

Copyright Teacher's Pet Publications 1996
11504 Hammock Point
Berlin MD 21811

Only the student materials in this unit plan (such as worksheets,
study questions, and tests) may be reproduced multiple times
for use in the purchaser's classroom.

For any additional copyright questions,
contact Teacher's Pet Publications.

www.tpet.com

TABLE OF CONTENTS - *Jacob Have I Loved*

Introduction	5
Unit Objectives	8
Reading Assignment Sheet	9
Unit Outline	10
Study Questions (Short Answer)	13
Quiz/Study Questions (Multiple Choice)	26
Pre-reading Vocabulary Worksheets	49
Lesson One (Introductory Lesson)	67
Nonfiction Assignment Sheet	70
Oral Reading Evaluation Form	84
Writing Assignment 1	69
Writing Assignment 2	85
Writing Assignment 3	94
Project	88
Writing Evaluation Form	76
Vocabulary Review Activities	102
Extra Writing Assignments/Discussion ?s	95
Unit Review Activities	104
Unit Tests	107
Unit Resource Materials	145
Vocabulary Resource Materials	163

A FEW NOTES ABOUT THE AUTHOR
KATHERINE PATERSON

PATERSON, Katherine (1932-). Three time Newbery award winning author Katherine Paterson calls herself a gypsy. She has lived in three countries and many states. She doesn't feel she has a home in that sense, so to her, she doesn't have a place out of which stories naturally come.

These sentiments come from an author whose writing in every aspect, not only setting, seems to come very naturally. Characters in Paterson's Newbery Honor book *The Great Gilly Hopkins* and Newbery Medal novels *Bridge to Terabithia* and *Jacob Have I Loved* totally belong where they are. And where they are is where she has spent a good part of her life, in the mid-Atlantic region of the United States. These are her recent works, though. Earlier novels: *The Sign of the Chrysanthemum, Of Nightingales That Weep, and The Master Puppeteer* are set in Japan, where she attended and taught school in the 1950's.

She doesn't think you have to fight dragons to write books, but to live deeply the life you've been given. Her deeply-lived life has taken her all over the world. She spent her early childhood in China, where her father was a missionary. During World War II, she was evacuated with her family. They came to live in various parts of Virginia, North Carolina, and West Virginia, where Katherine's odd clothes and British accent made her an outcast. As a result, she became an avid reader with a vivid imagination.

Katherine feels a book always grows out of who you are. You may wish it to be different, you might even pretend it to be different, but she insists the book will betray you. What you are will always come out in the book, she testifies. When asked what qualifies her to be a writer for children, she responds with the fact the she was once a weird little kid. She thinks that gives her a head start.

Katherine has written a total of twelve books including these most recent: *Lyddie* (1991), *The King's Equal* (1992), and *Flip-Flop Girl* (1994). She and her Presbyterian minister husband, John Paterson, have four children who have provided her with much of the subject matter for her keenly observant stories of family life. She presently lives in Barre, Vermont.

INTRODUCTION

This unit has been designed to develop students' reading, writing, thinking, and language skills through exercises and activities related to *Jacob Have I Loved* by Katherine Paterson. It includes twenty lessons, supported by extra resource materials.

The **introductory lesson** introduces students to background information about places, people, and events mentioned throughout this novel. It also doubles as the first writing assignment for the unit. Following the introductory activity, students are given an explanation of how the activity relates to the book they are about to read. Following the transition, students are given the materials they will be using during the unit.

The **reading assignments** are approximately thirty pages each; some are a little shorter while others are a little longer. Students have approximately 15 minutes of pre-reading work to do prior to each reading assignment. This pre-reading work involves reviewing the study questions for the assignment and doing some vocabulary work for 8 to 10 vocabulary words they will encounter in their reading.

The **study guide questions** are fact-based questions; students can find the answers to these questions right in the text. These questions come in two formats: short answer or multiple choice. The best use of these materials is probably to use the short answer version of the questions as study guides for students (since answers will be more complete), and to use the multiple choice version for occasional quizzes. It might be a good idea to make transparencies of your answer keys for the overhead projector.

The **vocabulary work** is intended to enrich students' vocabularies as well as to aid in the students' understanding of the book. Prior to each reading assignment, students will complete a two-part worksheet for approximately 8 to 10 vocabulary words in the upcoming reading assignment. Part I focuses on students' use of general knowledge and contextual clues by giving the sentence in which the word appears in the text. Students are then to write down what they think the words mean based on the words' usage. Part II nails down the definitions of the words by giving students dictionary definitions of the words and having students match the words to the correct definitions based on the words' contextual usage. Students should then have an understanding of the words when they meet them in the text.

After each reading assignment, students will go back and formulate answers for the study guide questions. Discussion of these questions serves as a **review** of the most important events and ideas presented in the reading assignments.

After students complete extra discussion questions, there is a **vocabulary review** lesson which pulls together all of the fragmented vocabulary lists for the reading assignments and gives students a review of all of the words they have studied.

Following the reading of the book, three lessons are devoted to the **extra discussion questions/writing assignments/activities**. These questions focus on interpretation, critical analysis and personal response, employing a variety of thinking skills and adding to the students' understanding of the novel. These questions are done as a **group activity**. Using the information they have acquired so far through individual work and class discussions, students get together to further examine the text and to brainstorm ideas relating to the themes of the novel.

The group activity is followed by a **reports and discussion/ activity** session in which the groups share their ideas about the book with the entire class; thus, the entire class gets exposed to many different ideas regarding the themes and events of the book.

There are three **writing assignments** in this unit, each with the purpose of informing, persuading, or having students express personal opinions. The first assignment is to inform: students write a composition about one of the background topics assigned in Lesson One. The second assignment is to give students a chance to persuade: students will pretend to be Sara Louise Bradshaw and write a persuasive letter to Captain Hiram Wallace convincing him that she equally deserves his widow Trudy's legacy as does her sister Caroline. The third assignment gives students the opportunity to express their personal ideas: students will interview their parents and/or relatives for information regarding their births. They will then write a personal account of the story of their birth.

The **nonfiction reading assignment** is tied in with Writing Assignment 1 and the introductory lesson. Students are required to read a piece of nonfiction related in some way to *Jacob Have I Loved*. In this case, the topics are assigned in Lesson One. After reading their nonfiction pieces, students will fill out a worksheet on which they answer questions regarding facts, interpretation, criticism, and personal opinions. During one class period, students make **oral presentations** about the nonfiction pieces they have read. This not only exposes all students to a wealth of information, it also gives students the opportunity to practice **public speaking**.

There is an optional **class project** (Save the Bay) through which students will gain first-hand knowledge of the challenges facing the Chesapeake Bay and have the opportunity to take part in helping to do something about these problems. This conservation project can be applied towards any watershed area; all activities are universal.

The **review lesson** pulls together all of the aspects of the unit. The teacher is given four or five choices of activities or games to use which all serve the same basic function of reviewing all of the information presented in the unit.

The **unit test** comes in two formats: all multiple choice-matching-true/false or with a mixture of matching, short answer, and composition. As a convenience, two different tests for each format have been included.

There are additional **support materials** included with this unit. The **unit resource section** includes suggestions for an in-class library, crossword and word search puzzles related to the novel, and extra vocabulary games and worksheets. There is a list of **bulletin board ideas** which gives the teacher suggestions for bulletin boards to go along with this unit. In addition, there is a list of **extra class activities** the teacher could choose from to enhance the unit or as a substitution for an exercise the teacher might feel is inappropriate for his/her class. **Answer keys** are located directly after the **reproducible student materials** throughout the unit. The student materials may be reproduced for use in the teacher's classroom without infringement of copyrights. No other portion of this unit may be reproduced without the written consent of Teacher's Pet Publications, Inc.

UNIT OBJECTIVES *Jacob Have I Loved*

1. Through reading Katherine Paterson's *Jacob Have I Loved*, students will recognize the trials of adolescence and be able to see jealousy's (primarily sibling rivalry's) effect on self-esteem.

2. Students will demonstrate their understanding of the text on four levels: factual, interpretive, critical and personal.

3. Students will gain an understanding of the comparison the author presents between the two twins and that of the Biblical twins, Jacob and Esau.

4. Students will define their own viewpoints on the aforementioned themes.

5. Students will gain appreciation for and demonstrate proficiency in identifying and using figurative language.

6. Students will do background research to make life on the Chesapeake Bay during the World War II era more meaningful.

7. Students will be given the opportunity to practice reading aloud and silently to improve their skills in each area.

8. Students will answer questions to demonstrate their knowledge and understanding of the main events and characters in *Jacob Have I Loved* as they relate to the author's theme development.

9. Students will enrich their vocabularies and improve their understanding of the novel through the vocabulary lessons prepared for use in conjunction with the novel.

10. The writing assignments in this unit are geared to several purposes:
    a. To have students demonstrate their abilities to inform, to persuade, or to express their own personal ideas
        Note: Students will demonstrate ability to write effectively to <u>inform</u> by developing and organizing facts to convey information. Students will demonstrate the ability to write effectively to <u>persuade</u> by selecting and organizing relevant information, establishing an argumentative purpose, and by designing an appropriate strategy for an identified audience. Students will demonstrate the ability to write effectively to <u>express personal ideas</u> by selecting a form and its appropriate elements.
    b. To check the students' reading comprehension
    c. To make students think about the ideas presented by the novel
    d. To encourage logical thinking
    e. To provide an opportunity to practice good grammar and improve students' use of the English language.

READING ASSIGNMENT SHEET - *Jacob Have I Loved*

Date Assigned	Reading Assignment (Chapters)	Completion Date
	Rass Island, 1, 2	
	3, 4	
	5, 6	
	7, 8, 9	
	10, 11, 12	
	13, 14	
	15, 16	
	17, 18	
	19, 20	

UNIT OUTLINE - *Jacob Have I Loved*

1 Library Writing Assignment #1	2 Introduction Read Rass Island PVR Ch 1,2	3 Study? Rass Island-Ch.2 PVR Ch. 3,4	4 Study? Ch. 3,4 PVR Ch. 5,6	5 Study ? Ch. 5,6 Writing Conference PVR Ch. 7-9
6 Study ? Ch. 7-9 PVR Ch. 10-12	7 Group Activity Figurative Language	8 Study ? Ch. 10-12 PV Ch. 13,14	9 Read Ch. 13,14 Writing Assignment #2	10 Study? Ch. 13,14 PVR Ch. 15,16
11 Study? Ch. 15,16 PVR Ch. 17,18	12 Study? Ch. 17,18 PV Ch. 19,20	13 Read Ch. 19,20 Study ? Ch 19,20	14 Writing Assignment #3	15 Extra Discussion Questions
16 Extra Discussion Questions	17 Extra Discussion Questions/ Activities	18 Vocabulary Review	19 Review	20 Test
21 Project Save the Bay	22	23	24	

Key: P = Preview Study Questions   V = Vocabulary Work   R = Read

STUDY GUIDE QUESTIONS

SHORT ANSWER STUDY GUIDE QUESTIONS - *Jacob Have I Loved*

Rass Island, Chapters 1,2
1. Where is Rass Island located?
2. Describe the island from the speaker's point of view.
3. What do the watermen's boats look like and for whom are they named?
4. Give the year this story begins.
5. Describe McCall Purnell.
6. Who is Sara Louise Bradshaw?
7. Why does Call go crabbing with Wheeze?
8. What is a "Jimmy"?
9. What is a "sook"?
10. How does Wheeze's Grandma react to her return?
11. In what way does her mother praise her efforts?
12. What does Wheeze's twin sister Caroline plan to write?
13. How did Mr. and Mrs. Bradshaw get together?
14. What do sons represent on Rass?
15. How does the story of their birth make Wheeze feel?
16. Where does Mrs. Bradshaw take Caroline as a ten day old baby?
17. When do the watermen tong for oysters?
18. During which months do they crab?
19. For what does Wheeze pray?
20. What musical instrument are the Bradshaws the first to own?
21. What is Caroline's true gift?
22. On whom does Wheeze blame her unhappiness?

Chapters 3,4
1. What event did Wheeze hear about on the radio Sunday, December 7, 1941?
2. How does the family react to the news?
3. What suggestion does Wheeze make to Mr. Rice at school?
4. How does her teacher respond?
5. What's different about Caroline's performance at this year's Christmas concert?
6. In Wheeze's daydream, what does she have Caroline do?
7. Name Grandma's two stock phrases.
8. Why did the women of Rass hate the water?
9. Why does Wheeze take the wagon down to the ferry?
10. What does Caroline do in public that embarrasses Wheeze?
11. Describe the stranger who debarks the ferry.
12. Where do they bury their dead on Rass? Why?
13. What sparks the Bradshaw's interest on their way home from the ferry?

Short Answer Study Guide Questions - *Jacob Have I Loved* Page 2

Chapters 5,6
1. Who does Grandma think the stranger is?
2. What story emerges from the past about Hiram Wallace?
3. Wheeze is convinced the stranger is actually what?
4. Explain how the islanders purchased shoes.
5. To what did the Captain compare Wheeze and Call's names?
6. Give examples of the Captain's wit.
7. Whom does the Captain prefer?
8. For what reason does Wheeze fly into a wounded rage at Caroline?
9. What does Wheeze search for in the Bible?
10. How does Wheeze plan to leave the island?
11. Share Call's reaction to Wheeze's poetry.

Chapters 7-9
1. Which of the Ten Commandments did Wheeze wrongly accuse the Captain of breaking?
2. Does the Captain pay Call and Wheeze for helping him every day?
3. According to Wheeze, which two months of the year are the worst?
4. How does Wheeze respond to the letter from LYRICS UNLIMITED?
5. What does the Captain say that finally gets Wheeze to laugh?
6. When Wheeze returns the orange tom cat to Auntie Braxton's what does she find?
7. How does the Captain confirm himself as the 'real' Hiram Wallace?
8. What unknown fact about Trudy does the Captain share with Call and Wheeze?
9. How does Wheeze feel about the Captain's plan to drown Trudy's cats?
10. What is Caroline's cat plan?

Chapters 10-12
1. How do the Bradshaws prepare for the storm?
2. Why does Truitt waken Wheeze at the onset of the storm?
3. How does Grandma behave during the storm?
4. Who suffered the most damage from the storm?
5. What action does Wheeze take to comfort the Captain?
6. In what way does Mr. Bradshaw help out the Captain?
7. Why does Wheeze want to throw a jar of green beans at Grandma?
8. Why does Wheeze study people's hands?
9. What does Caroline do that terribly upsets Wheeze?

Short Answer Study Guide Questions - *Jacob Have I Loved* Page 3

Chapters 13, 14
1. How does Wheeze see herself at the beginning of the chapter?
2. What is Caroline's solution to Hiram's living arrangement problem?
3. How does Wheeze feel about the plan?
4. Why are Wheeze and Call shocked while dining with Trudy and Hiram?
5. For what reason does Wheeze abruptly leave their home?
6. Why does Wheeze become jealous of Call?
7. The Captain brings what news that causes Wheeze to feel betrayed?

Chapters 15, 16
1. Grandma taunts Sara Louise with a verse from the Bible, " As it is written, Jacob have I loved, Esau have I hated until Wheeze does what? What does it mean?
2. Where does Caroline go?
3. Why does Call leave?
4. Rather than attend school with Caroline and Call gone, what does Wheeze now do?
5. Who home teaches her?
6. Wheeze feels great empathy for the sooks. Of whom is she thinking?
7. How does Wheeze fare on her graduation exams?
8. Call's return for a visit brings some startling news for Wheeze. What was it?

Chapters 17, 18
1. Where do Mr. and Mrs. Bradshaw go without Wheeze or Grandma?
2. How does Wheeze spend Christmas?
3. What information does Grandma share with Wheeze that surprises her?
4. Why does the Captain say, "Youth is a mortal wound"?
5. What information about herself does Wheeze share with the Captain?
6. Why does Grandma whack Wheeze on the side of her head with her Bible?
7. While washing widows with her mother, why does Wheeze become so furious?
8. What one word of her mother's allows her to finally leave the island ?

Chapters 19, 20
1. Why does Sara Louise leave the University of Maryland?
2. Where does she transfer?
3. Why does she choose a town named Truitt, Virginia to begin her career?
4. What does she compare this mountain-locked valley to?
5. Name the most pressing health problem in Truitt.
6. When did she know that she would marry Joseph Wojtkiewicz?
7. Who goes in Wheeze's place to her father's funeral? Why?
8. How does Wheeze treat the twin babies she delivers?

ANSWER KEY: SHORT ANSWER STUDY QUESTIONS *Jacob Have I Loved*

Rass Island, Chapter 1,2
1. Where is Rass Island located?
    Rass Island is located in the Chesapeake Bay near Crisfield, Maryland.

2. Describe the island from the speaker's point of view.
    It is a low lying island on the faded olive water of the Chesapeake with a church and cluster of white board houses being the first sight from the ferry. Mazes of docks, each with an islander's skipjack tied to it dot the harbor. Near the ferry house is Kellam's General Store, painted green and housing the post office. Behind it are the houses with their picket fences. The village only covers one-third of the island, the rest is salt marsh.

3. What do the watermen's boats look like and for whom are they named?
    Each has a small cabin toward the bow, washboards wide enough for a man to stand on running from the point of the bow to the stern. Near the winch that pulls the line of pots up from the Bay bottom is a large washtub into which all the harvest is deposited and then sorted. Each boat bears a woman's name, usually the waterman's mother or grandmother, depending on how long the boat has been in the family.

4. Give the year this story begins.
    This story begins in the summer of 1941.

5. Describe McCall Purnell.
    "Call" is fourteen years old, pudgy, bespectacled, and totally unsentimental.

6. Who is Sara Louise Bradshaw?
    "Wheeze" is a thirteen-year old twin who is tall and large boned, with delusions of beauty and romance. She and Call go crabbing weekday mornings.

7. Why does Call go crabbing with Wheeze?
    His father is dead and he has no man to take him on board a regular crab boat.

8. What is a "Jimmy"?
    A Jimmy is a male blue crab.

9. What is a "sook"?
    A sook is a grown-up lady blue crab.

10. How does Wheeze's Grandma react to her return?
    Her Grandma says she is a mess and has ruined every scrap of clothes she owns.

11. In what way does her mother praise her efforts?
    Her mother beams at her and says she had a "good" morning.

12. What does Wheeze's twin sister Caroline plan to write?
    Caroline decides to write a book about her life, because once she becomes famous, information like that is very valuable.

13. How did Mr. and Mrs. Bradshaw get together?
    Mrs. Bradshaw came to Rass to teach in the island school. Mr. Bradshaw was recovering from a war wound and they fell in love.

14. What do sons represent on Rass?
    Sons represent wealth on Rass.

15. How does the story of their birth make Wheeze feel?
    She feels cold all over, as though she was the newborn infant a second time, cast aside and forgotten.

16. Where does Mrs. Bradshaw take Caroline as a ten day old baby?
    She takes the failing infant Caroline, by ferry, to the hospital in Crisfield.

17. When do the watermen tong for oysters?
    They tong for oysters from November to March.

18. During which months do they crab?
    The watermen crab from late April to the fall.

19. For what does Wheeze pray for?
    She prays to turn into a boy so she can join her father on his skipjack.

20. What musical instrument are the Bradshaws the first to own?
    They are the sole island owners of a piano.

21. What is Caroline's true gift?
    Caroline's true gift is her voice.

22. On whom does Wheeze blame her unhappiness?
    She blames her unhappiness on Caroline, her grandmother, her mother, and even herself.

Chapters 3, 4

1. What event did Wheeze hear about on the radio Sunday, December 7, 1941?
    She heard the announcement of the Japanese bombing of the American fleet at Pearl Harbor.

2. How does the family react to the news?
    They stood shocked, huddled together before the radio set.

3. What suggestion does Wheeze make to Mr. Rice at school?
    She suggests they cancel the Christmas program due to all the suffering and dying.

4. How does her teacher respond?
    He says thousands were suffering and dying when Christ was born and he continues the Christmas program practice.

5. What's different about Caroline's performance at this year's Christmas concert?
    She performs a different solo than her usual," O Holy Night". She sings "I Wonder as I Wander," a piercingly beautiful song, which only she could sing to perfection.

6. In Wheeze's daydream, what does she have Caroline do?
    She dreams a giant hand descends from the sky and shoves Caroline to her knees and demands she no longer call her by her nickname, Wheeze, but call her Sara Louise.

7. Name Grandma's two stock phrases.
    Grandma's two stock phrases are: "I hate the water" and "I love the Lord."

8. Why do the women of Rass hate the water?
    The island women see the water as the wild, untamed kingdom of their men and they try to resist its power over them.

9. Why does Wheeze take the wagon down to the ferry?
    Wheeze takes the wagon to help her mother bring back the groceries.

10. What does Caroline do in public that embarrasses Wheeze?
    Caroline kisses her father on the cheek.

11. Describe the stranger who debarks the ferry.
    The stranger is an old man with the strong, stocky build of a waterman. His hair, under his seaman's cap, is white and thick and hangs halfway down his neck. He has a full, white mustache and beard, and is wearing a heavy overcoat. He is carrying a valise, and has two more ancient bags and a trunk with him.

12. Where do they bury their dead on Rass? Why?
    They bury their dead in their front yards due to the scarcity of high ground.

13. What sparks the Bradshaw's interest on their way home from the ferry?
    The stranger swiftly overtakes them on their walk home and continues to walk ahead past them.

Chapters 5,6
1. Who does Grandma think the stranger is?
    She, and all islanders over fifty, think he is Hiram Wallace, a former islander.

2. What story emerges from the past about Hiram Wallace?
    The old people told the story that Captain Wallace and his son, Hiram, had let down their sails and were waiting out a storm in the bay, using the sail for protection. Hiram feared lightening would strike the tall mast of his father's skipjack, so he rushed out from under his sail cover, took an axe, and chopped the mast to the level of the deck. They were sighted drifting mastless on the bay after the storm, and were towed home. When everyone found out what he had done, he became the butt of all the watermen's jokes and left the island.

3. Wheeze is convinced the stranger is actually what?
    She imagines he could be a spy observing the Norfolk warships in the Bay.

4. Explain how the islanders purchase shoes.
    They stand on a piece of brown wrapping paper and draw a pencil line around both of their feet. These outlines are then sent to Sears Roebuck's mail-order house and they send shoes to fit.

5. To what did the Captain compare Wheeze and Call's names?
    The Captain says they sound like a vaudeville act.

6. Give examples of the Captain's wit.
    He tells them Wheeze and Cough would be an even better name for them. He tells Call that if he wants him he will just call 'Call."

7. Whom does the Captain prefer?
   The Captain appears to prefer Call.

8. For what reason does Wheeze fly into a wounded rage at Caroline?
   She resents Caroline's remarks about how dirty her fingernails are after a day of crabbing.

9. What does Wheeze search for in the Bible?
   She searches for some shred of evidence that she will not be eternally damned for hating her sister.

10. How does Wheeze plan to leave the island?
    Wheeze plans to double her crab catch and keep half the money for herself, as well as make money on her poetry. She will then have enough cash to leave and attend boarding school in Crisfield.

11. Share Call's reaction to Wheeze's poetry.
    He is confused and thinks it is dumb.

Chapters 7-9

1. Which of the Ten Commandments did Wheeze wrongly accuse the Captain of breaking?
   Wheeze wrongfully accuses him of breaking the Seventh Commandment. She thought it was the one about working on the Sabbath. She was mistaken, it was the one on adultery.

2. Does the Captain pay Call and Wheeze for helping him every day?
   The Captain offers, but Call refuses for both of them.

3. According to Wheeze, which two months of the year are the worst?
   She claims February and August are the worst two months of the year on the island.

4. How does Wheeze respond to the letter from LYRICS UNLIMITED?
   She is heartsick, rips it up, and flings it into the bay.

5. What does the Captain say that finally gets Wheeze to laugh?
   Wheeze laughs when the Captain tells Call there isn't any commandment about how to speak to tom cats.

6. When Wheeze returns the orange tom cat to Auntie Braxton's what does she find?
   She sees Auntie Braxton lying on the front room floor with cats crawling all over her.

7. How does the Captain confirm himself as the *real* Hiram Wallace?
    He used Auntie Braxton's first name, Trudy, when addressing her. No one has called her that since she was a young woman.

8. What unknown fact about Trudy does the Captain share with Call and Wheeze?
    Trudy' father had left her quite a sum of cash.

9. How does Wheeze feel about the Captain's plan to drown Trudy's cats?
    She is strongly opposed and jumps out of the boat, swimming for shore.

10. What is Caroline's cat plan?
    Caroline proposes they drug the cats with paregoric, and take them door to door to give them away. It is successful.

Chapters 10-12

1. How do the Bradshaws prepare for the storm?
    They boarded up the windows, carried the canned goods upstairs, and the father sank his boat.

2. Why does Truitt waken Wheeze at the onset of the storm?
    He wants her to go down and get the Captain for fear the storm will get worse.

3. How does Grandma behave during the storm?
    She rocks in her rocking chair and cries out, quoting scripture.

4. Who suffered the most damage from the storm?
    The Captain loses everything.

5. What action does Wheeze take to comfort the Captain?
    She is so sorry for him that she put her arms around him.

6. In what way does Mr. Bradshaw help out the Captain?
    He extends him the offer to stay with them temporarily.

7. Why does Wheeze want to throw a jar of green beans at Grandma?
    She is upset because her Grandmother notices her attraction to the old man and quotes scripture about it.

8. Why does Wheeze study people's hands?
    She becomes obsessed with the cleanliness and neatness of the Captain's hands and nails. She feels they are the most revealing part of the human body.

9. What does Caroline do that terribly upsets Wheeze?
   Wheeze discovers Caroline using her Jergen's lotion which she had hidden in her drawers.

Chapters 13, 14

1. How does Wheeze see herself at the beginning of the chapter?
   Wheeze imagines herself going crazy.

2. What is Caroline's solution to Hiram's living arrangement problem?
   Caroline proposes Hiram marry Trudy and then he may stay at her house with her.

3. How does Wheeze feel about the plan?
   She hates the idea and tells Caroline she'll kill her if she mentions it.

4. Why are Wheeze and Call shocked while dining with Trudy and Hiram?
   Hiram offers them wine. Caroline is the only one who partakes.

5. For what reason does Wheeze abruptly leave their home?
   After Wheeze fails to laugh at a humorous story the Captain told, Caroline told Trudy not to mind Wheeze, "she doesn't think anything's funny." Wheeze reacted violently, while Call and Caroline laughed it off. She couldn't stand it when the Captain kindly questioned her.

6. Why does Wheeze become jealous of Call?
   Call's family is destitute and Wheeze's father takes him aboard the *Portia Sue* as an oyster culler.

7. The Captain brings what news that causes Wheeze to feel betrayed?
   He joyfully brought the news that he had investigated how much a good music boarding school in Baltimore would cost for Caroline, and Trudy's legacy would be enough to cover it.

Chapters 15, 16

1. Grandma taunts Sara Louise with a verse from the Bible, " As it is written, Jacob have I loved, but Esau have I hated" until Wheeze does what? What does it mean?
   Wheeze goes to the Bible and locates the verse to determine who says it. From Romans, the ninth chapter and the thirteenth verse she finds that it is God who says it. She feels that God himself hates her too. The Biblical tale is one in which Esau, the elder twin is cheated out his birthright by his conniving brother Jacob, and their mother Rebecca. Wheeze has hated this story from childhood.

2. Where does Caroline go?
   Caroline leaves the island to go to music school in Baltimore, compliments of Trudy Braxton's legacy.

3. Why does Call leave?
   Call has enlisted in the U.S. Navy.

4. Rather than attend school with Caroline and Call gone, what does Wheeze now do?
   Wheeze now, little by little, takes on more responsibility with her father's crabbing and oystering business. She ultimately goes out on the *Portia Sue* with him daily.

5. Who home teaches her?
   Her mother and the Captain.

6. While sorting crabs, Wheeze feels great empathy for the sooks. Of whom is she thinking?
   She feels the male crabs have more of a chance to live, but the female crabs, ordinary, ungifted ones, just get soft and die. She is thinking of herself.

7. How does Wheeze fare on her graduation exams?
   Wheeze scores the highest grades recorded from Rass Island.

8. Call's return for a visit brings some startling news for Wheeze. What was it?
   Call has proposed marriage to her twin sister, Caroline.

Chapters 17, 18

1. Where do Mr. and Mrs. Bradshaw go without Wheeze or Grandma?
   Wheeze's parents go to New York for Call and Caroline's wedding.

2. How does Wheeze spend Christmas?
   She stays home tending to Grandma while her parents are gone. She invites Hiram over to have Christmas dinner with them.

3. What information does Grandma share with Wheeze that surprises her?
   Grandma discloses that when she was a young girl she was in love with Hiram, although he was somewhat older.

4. Why does the Captain say, "Youth is a mortal wound?"
   The Captain is trying to explain how painful being young can be and that it is "good" to be old.

5. What information about herself does Wheeze share with the Captain?
   Wheeze shares her ambition to become a doctor with the Captain.

6. Why does Grandma whack Wheeze on the side of her head with her Bible?
   Wheeze quotes a passage from Proverbs in the Bible about living in a house with a contentious woman, sweetly, to her in response to her Grandmother's rantings about her mother. She gained satisfaction from doing it, and knew she deserved the punishment.

7. While washing windows with her mother, why does Wheeze become so furious?
   Wheeze discovers that her mother used to write poetry and wanted to go to Paris, but instead came to Rass to teach. It is an insult to Wheeze to think her mother chose the life she leads on the island over something far more stimulating.

8. What one word of her mother's allows her to finally leave the island?
   Her mother tells her if she leaves the island her father and she will miss her. Wheeze asks if they will miss her as much as they miss Caroline. Her mother responds with, "More."

Chapters 19, 20
1. Why does Sara Louise leave the University of Maryland?
   Her advisor urges her to switch to nursing because now that the war is over, all the returning veterans will be favored for medical school, especially over a female.
2. Where does she transfer?
   She transfers to the University of Kentucky.

3. Why does she choose a town named Truitt, Virginia to begin her career?
   It is in the mountains and it is her father's name.

4. What does she compare this mountain-locked valley to?
   She compares it to an island. The Appalachian wilderness is like an island's water, and their jeeps are like the boats on Rass.

5. Name the most pressing health problem in Truitt.
   The valley men get drunk on Saturday nights and beat their wives and children.

6. When did she know that she would marry Joseph Wojtkiewicz?
     She came to his house to care for his ill child. After she was done, he questioned
     her about herself. After she shared, he said, "God in heaven's been raising you for
     this valley from the day you were born." He then smiled. He reminded her of the
     kind of man that would sing to the oysters, like her father.

7. Who goes in Wheeze's place to her father's funeral? Why?
     Joseph, her husband goes because she is nine months pregnant.

8. How does Wheeze treat the twin babies she delivers?
     She wants to give equal attention to both babies, but the smaller one requires more.
     She is stricken with the realization that she has forgotten the healthier one, the boy,
     who is resting alone in the basket. She admonishes the family to hold him, the first
     born, as well as the smaller, frailer girl.

MULTIPLE CHOICE STUDY GUIDE/QUIZ QUESTIONS- *Jacob Have I Loved*

Rass Island, Chapters 1,2

1. Rass Island is located in
   a. Bay of Biscay
   b. Cape Cod
   c. Chesapeake Bay
   d. Hawaii

2. The island is described as
   a. having lots of docks and boats
   b. a salt marsh
   c. one-third of the land is village
   d. all of the above

3. What do the watermen's boats look like and for whom are they named?
   a. They have a small cabin.
   b. They have wide side washboards.
   c. They have barrels and buckets lying around.
   d. They are named for the women of the family.
   e. all of the above

4. This story begins in the year
   a. 1942
   b. 1948
   c. 1941
   d. 1952

5. McCall Purnell is
   a. thin and wiry
   b. preppy
   c. intellectual
   d. pudgy and bespectacled

6. Sara Louise Bradshaw is
   a. Call's sister
   b. local school teacher
   c. a twin nicknamed "Wheeze"
   d. a cousin of Call's

Study Guide/Quiz Questions- *Jacob Have I Loved* Multiple Choice Format Page 2

7. Call goes crabbing with Wheeze because
    a. he has no father
    b. he is bored over the summer
    c. his boat broke down
    d. she bribed him

8. A "Jimmy" is
    a. a female blue crab
    b. a male blue crab
    c. an oyster
    d. a Chevrolet truck

9. A "sook" is
    a. a male blue crab
    b. a female oyster
    c. something you hang your coat on
    d. a lady crab

10. Grandma reacts to Wheeze's return by
    a. smiling at her
    b. nagging her
    c. kissing and hugging her
    d. ignoring her

11. Her mother praised her efforts by
    a. patting her on the back
    b. offering her money
    c. smiling and saying "good day"
    d. sending her to her room

12. Wheeze's twin sister, Caroline, plans to write
    a. her autobiography
    b. a novel about the island
    c. a children's story about crabbing
    d. a biography of F.D.R.

Study Guide/Quiz Questions- *Jacob Have I Loved* Multiple Choice Format Page 3

13. Mr. and Mrs. Bradshaw got together when
    a. they met on the ferry
    b. she came to be the island school teacher
    c. he fought in World War I, and she was his nurse
    d. they ran into each other in Ocean City on a vacation

14. On Rass, sons represent
    a. fame and fortune
    b. wealth
    c. disgrace
    d. acceptance

15. The story of their birth makes Wheeze feel
    a. nostalgic
    b. warm and cozy
    c. cold and neglected

16. Mrs. Bradshaw takes Caroline as a ten day old baby
    a. to the hospital
    b. to Crisfield
    c. on the ferry
    d. all of the above

17. The watermen tong for oysters
    a. from February to June
    b. from November to March
    c. from January to May
    d. from April to September

18. The watermen crab
    a. all winter
    b. in the summer only
    c. in the fall and winter both
    d. spring, summer, and fall

Study Guide/Quiz Questions- *Jacob Have I Loved* Multiple Choice Format Page 4

19. Wheeze prays
    a. to lose weight
    b. to become a boy
    c. to be prettier
    d. to be able to sing like Caroline

20. The Bradshaws own the first island
    a. violin
    b. organ
    c. piano
    d. radio

21. Caroline's true gift is
    a. her voice
    b. her acting ability
    c. her piano playing
    d. her artistic ability

22. Wheeze blames her unhappiness on
    a. herself
    b. her Grandma
    c. Caroline
    d. her mother
    e. her father
    f. a-d

Study Guide/Quiz Questions- *Jacob Have I Loved* Multiple Choice Format Page 5

Chapters 3, 4

1. Wheeze hears about what event on the radio Sunday, December 7, 1941?
    a. V-J Day
    b. Pearl Harbor
    c. Hitler's death
    d. F.D.R.'s death

2. The family reacts to the news by being
    a. overjoyed
    b. relieved
    c. nervous
    d. stunned

3. Wheeze suggests to Mr. Rice at school that they
    a. cancel Christmas
    b. go Christmas carolling
    c. join the Navy
    d. volunteer for the Salvation Army

4. He responds by
    a. agreeing with her
    b. ignoring her
    c. dismissing her suggestion and continuing practice
    d. deciding to take a class vote

5. What's different about Caroline's performance at this year's Christmas concert?
    a. She wears a halo.
    b. She directs the choir.
    c. She has a different solo than last year.
    d. She catches a cold and can't sing at all.

6. In Wheeze's daydream, she has Caroline
    a. be her servant
    b. call her by her real name, Sara Louise
    c. move out of their bedroom
    d. cull the oysters

Study Guide/Quiz Questions- *Jacob Have I Loved* Multiple Choice Format Page 6

7. Grandma's two stock phrases are
   a. I love the water
   b. I hate the water
   c. I love the Lord
   d. both b and c

8. The women of Rass hate the water because
   a. they can't see the bottom
   b. of the sharks
   c. they can't swim
   d. they resent its power over them

9. Wheeze takes the wagon down to the ferry to
   a. fill it up with crabs
   b. load it with clothes
   c. bring back the groceries
   d. haul Grandma home

10. What does Caroline do in public that embarrasses Wheeze?
    a. She kisses their father.
    b. She winks at Call.
    c. She wears a skirt above her knees.
    d. She sings loudly.

11. The stranger who debarks the ferry is
    a. stocky and old with a white beard and mustache
    b. middle-aged with two children
    c. thin and frail
    d. young and handsome

12. They bury their dead on Rass in
    a. the churchyard
    b. a cemetery
    c. their front yards
    d. their back yards

Study Guide/Quiz Questions- *Jacob Have I Loved* Multiple Choice Format Page 7

13. What sparks the Bradshaw's interest on their way home from the ferry?
       a. The sky clouds up.
       b. German airplanes fly overhead.
       c. Grandma collapses.
       d. The stranger walks past them.

Study Guide/Quiz Questions- *Jacob Have I Loved* Multiple Choice Format Page 8

<u>Chapters 5,6</u>
1. Grandma thinks the stranger is
    a. Hiram Wallace
    b. a former islander
    c. dead Captain Wallace's son
    d. all of the above

2. What story emerges from the past about Hiram Wallace?
    a. He ran off on his wedding day.
    b. He fell off the ferry and had amnesia.
    c. He cut down his daddy's mast during a storm.
    d. He became a doctor and discovered a cure for malaria.

3. Wheeze is convinced the stranger is actually
    a. a German POW
    b. a spy for the Navy
    c. a counterspy
    d. an imposter

4. The islanders purchased shoes
    a. by going to Crisfield on the ferry
    b. by mail ordering from Sears Roebuck
    c. through a traveling salesman
    d. by sending their old shoes to Baltimore

5. The Captain compared Wheeze and Call's names to
    a. a pair of parrots
    b. a vaudeville act
    c. a disease
    d. an old friend from the war

6. The Captain demonstrates his wit by
    a. singing silly songs for them
    b. telling corny jokes about himself
    c. telling them tall tales
    d. none of the above

Study Guide/Quiz Questions- *Jacob Have I Loved* Multiple Choice Format Page 9

7. The Captain prefers
   a. Call
   b. Wheeze
   c. Susan
   d. Trudy

8. Wheeze flies into a wounded rage at Caroline because
   a. Caroline remarks how dirty her fingernails are.
   b. Caroline won't share dessert.
   c. Caroline borrows her best dress without asking.
   d. Caroline steals her boyfriend.

9. Wheeze searches in the Bible for
   a. the Lord's Prayer
   b. a Psalm to read to Grandma
   c. Proverbs
   d. evidence that she won't be damned for hating her sister

10. Wheeze plans to leave the island by
    a. taking the ferry
    b. making enough money to go to school in Crisfield
    c. running away one night
    d. swimming to the nearest sand bar and waiting for a boat to rescue her

11. Call thinks Wheeze's poetry is
    a. beautiful
    b. humorous
    c. dumb
    d. romantic

Study Guide/Quiz Questions- *Jacob Have I Loved* Multiple Choice Format Page 10

Chapters 7-9

1. Which of the Ten Commandments did Wheeze wrongly accuse the Captain of breaking?
    a. First
    b. Seventh
    c. Fifth
    d. Tenth

2. The Captain pays Call and Wheeze for helping him every day.
    a. true
    b. false

3. According to Wheeze, which two months of the year are the worst?
    a. July and August
    b. August and September
    c. January and February
    d. February and August

4. Wheeze responds to the letter from LYRICS UNLIMITED by
    a. writing back immediately
    b. tearing the letter into bits
    c. sending them money
    d. mailing them more poems

5. What does the Captain say that finally gets Wheeze to laugh?
    a. He tells Call to hush.
    b. He reminds them of the first time they met.
    c. He tells Call there's nothing in the Bible about how to talk to tom cats.
    d. He tells a joke about God thinking he's F.D.R.

6. Wheeze returns the orange tom cat to Auntie Braxton's and finds
    a. a new litter of kittens
    b. Auntie Braxton looking for the tom
    c. a deserted house
    d. Auntie Braxton lying on the floor with cats crawling all over her

Study Guide/Quiz Questions- *Jacob Have I Loved* Multiple Choice Format Page 11

7. The Captain confirms himself as the *real* Hiram Wallace by
   a. showing his identification
   b. locating his father's treasure
   c. calling Auntie Braxton by her first name
   d. reciting the waterman's pledge

8. The Captain shares with Call and Wheeze the secret about Trudy that
   a. she was once married to him
   b. she inherited a lot of money
   c. her house belongs to the church
   d. she is Catholic

9. How does Wheeze feel about the Captain's plan to drown Trudy's cats?
   a. agrees
   b. disagrees

10. What is Caroline's cat plan?
    a. drown them
    b. take them to the SPCA in Baltimore
    c. put them in crab pots
    d. drug them and hand them out door to door

Study Guide/Quiz Questions- *Jacob Have I Loved* Multiple Choice Format Page 12

Chapters 10-12

1. The Bradshaws prepare for the storm by
    a. bringing the canned goods upstairs
    b. boarding up the windows
    c. sinking the boat
    d. all of the above
    e. a and b

2. Truitt awakens Wheeze at the onset of the storm to
    a. help bring the canned goods upstairs
    b. take care of Grandma
    c. go get the Captain and bring him there
    d. none of the above

3. During the storm, Grandma
    a. sleeps
    b. cries out and rocks in her rocker
    c. reads the Bible
    d. runs and hides

4. Who suffered the most damage from the storm?
    a. Bradshaws
    b. Auntie Braxton
    c. Captain Wallace
    d. Captain Billy

5. To comfort the Captain, Wheeze
    a. embraces him
    b. gives him a present she has made
    c. smiles and pats him on the shoulder
    d. bails out his boat

6. Mr. Bradshaw helps out the Captain by
    a. lending him money
    b. offering their home to him
    c. taking him to the ferry
    d. giving him furniture

Study Guide/Quiz Questions- *Jacob Have I Loved* Multiple Choice Format Page 13

7. Wheeze wants to throw a jar of green beans at Grandma because
    a. Wheeze wants her bedroom
    b. Grandma notices her attraction to the Captain and quotes scripture about it
    c. Grandma won't take her nap
    d. Wheeze hates the dinner Grandma wants

8. Wheeze studies people's hands because
    a. she worries hers are damaged from crabbing
    b. she is going to paint a portrait of hands
    c. she thinks they reveal a person's true character
    d. she can't look them in the eye

9. What does Caroline do that terribly upsets Wheeze?
    a. Caroline uses her lotion without permission.
    b. Caroline takes her job.
    c. Caroline breaks into her piggy bank where she has stashed her hidden earnings.
    d. Caroline criticizes her once again.

Study Guide/Quiz Questions- *Jacob Have I Loved* Multiple Choice Format Page 14
Chapters 13, 14

1. At the beginning of the chapter, Wheeze sees herself as
   a. ready to leave the island
   b. a man
   c. crazy
   d. falling in love

2. Caroline's solution to Hiram's living arrangement problem is
   a. have him continue to stay with them
   b. have him marry Grandma
   c. to help him build a new house
   d. have him marry Trudy

3. How does Wheeze feel about the plan?
   a. agrees
   b. disagrees

4. Wheeze and Call are shocked while dining with Trudy and Hiram because
   a. Hiram kisses Trudy at the table.
   b. Trudy faints during dinner.
   c. Hiram gets drunk.
   d. Hiram offers them all a glass of wine.

5. Wheeze abruptly leaves their home because
   a. she feels sick
   b. she feels Caroline has insulted her in front of everyone
   c. Grandma needs her
   d. she can't be late for work

6. Wheeze becomes jealous of Call due to the fact that
   a. he is now working with her father
   b. he is able to live in his own place
   c. he joins the Navy
   d. he gets to go to Crisfield

7. What news does the Captain bring that causes Wheeze to feel betrayed?
   a. He will donate Trudy's legacy to the SPCA in Baltimore.
   b. Trudy left her money to the church.
   c. He wants to send Caroline to music school in Baltimore.
   d. He wants to adopt Call.

Study Guide/Quiz Questions- *Jacob Have I Loved* Multiple Choice Format Page 15

Chapters 15, 16
1. What does the scripture Grandma quotes to Wheeze mean to Wheeze?
	a. Esau hates Jacob
	b. God hates her
	c. God hates Jacob
	d. Jacob loves her

2. Caroline goes to
	a. Crisfield
	b. Washington
	c. New York City
	d. Baltimore

3. Call leaves to
	a. join the Navy
	b. follow Caroline
	c. run away to Canada

4. Rather than attend school with Caroline and Call gone, what does Wheeze now do?
	a. becomes a recluse
	b. works for Captain Billy
	c. works for her father
	d. babysits Grandma

5. Wheeze's home teachers are
	a. her mother
	b. Mr. Rice
	c. the Captain
	d. both a and c

6. While sorting crabs, Wheeze feels great empathy for the sooks. Of whom is she thinking?
	a. herself
	b. Grandma
	c. her mother

7. How does Wheeze fare on her graduation exams?
	a. scores the highest from Rass
	b. fails them
	c. doesn't take them
	d. barely passes

Study Guide/Quiz Questions- *Jacob Have I Loved* Multiple Choice Format Page 16

8. Call's return for a visit brings some startling news for Wheeze. What was it?
   a. He asks her to marry him.
   b. He was wounded in the South Pacific
   c. He has proposed to Caroline
   d. He has re-enlisted for another four years in the Navy

Study Guide/Quiz Questions - *Jacob Have I Loved* Multiple Choice Format Page 17

<u>Chapters 17,18</u>
1. Wheeze and Grandma stay home while Mr. and Mrs. Bradshaw go to
    a. a waterman's convention in Baltimore
    b. a war rally in Washington D.C.
    c. visit relatives in Virginia
    d. New York City to Caroline and Call's wedding

2. Wheeze spends Christmas
    a. working the water
    b. at home with Grandma and the Captain
    c. in New York City
    d. looking at colleges

3. What information does Grandma share with Wheeze that surprises her?
    a. She was once in love with Hiram.
    b. She had a daughter that died.
    c. She has not always hated the island.
    d. She has never been farther away than Crisfield.

4. Why does the Captain say, "Youth is a mortal wound?"
    a. He shot someone by mistake when he was young.
    b. He hates that he is old now.
    c. He wants to be young again.
    d. He's content to be old, rather than struggling with youth.

5. What aspiration does Wheeze share with the Captain?
    a. She loves Call.
    b. She has never seen the mountains.
    c. She wants to become a doctor.

6. Grandma whacks Wheeze on the side of her head with her Bible because
    a. Wheeze quotes scripture to her sarcastically.
    b. Wheeze's clothes are dirty from crabbing.
    c. Wheeze won't take her to the ferry.
    d. Wheeze ignores her.

7. Wheeze becomes furious while washing windows with her mother because
    a. she makes her do the neighbor's windows too
    b. she chose Rass over Paris
    c. she shares that she was married before
    d. Grandma is bossing them around and her mother just takes it

Study Guide/Quiz Questions- *Jacob Have I Loved* Multiple Choice Format Page 18

8. What one word of her mother's allows her to finally leave the island ?
        a. less
        b. yes
        c. more

Study Guide/Quiz Questions *Jacob Have I Loved* Multiple Choice Format Page 19

Chapters 19, 20
1. Sara Louise leaves the University of Maryland because
    a. she can't afford to attend anymore
    b. her father needs her to help him
    c. she fails out
    d. her advisor tells her to forget medical school

2. She transfers to
    a. U.M.B.C.
    b. Salisbury State College
    c. University of Kentucky
    d. Virginia Tech

3. Why does she choose a town named Truitt, Virginia to begin her career?
    a. It's far away from Rass.
    b. It bears her father's name.
    c. It's in the mountains.
    d. Both a and c

4. She compares this mountain-locked valley to
    a. a piece of heaven
    b. an island
    c. a dessert

5. The most pressing health problem in Truitt is
    a. influenza
    b. emphysema
    c. domestic violence

6. She knew that she would marry Joseph Wojtkiewicz when
    a. he kissed her
    b. he smiled
    c. his children climbed on her lap
    d. he proposed to her

Study Guide/Quiz Questions- *Jacob Have I Loved* Multiple Choice Format Page 20

7. Who goes in Wheeze's place to her father's funeral?
    a. Joseph
    b. Call
    c. Caroline
    d. Emily

8. How does Wheeze treat the twin babies she delivers?
    a. She gives more attention to the first-born boy.
    b. She is impatient and needs to get home.
    c. She treats them both equally.
    d. She gives more attention to the smaller, second-born baby girl.

ANSWER KEY- MULTIPLE CHOICE STUDY/QUIZ QUESTIONS
Jacob Have I Loved

Rass Island, Chapters 1,2		Chapters 3,4	Chapters 5,6	Chapters 7-9	Chapters 10-12	
1. c	14. b	1. b	1. d	1. b	1. d	2. d
	15. c	2. d	2. c	2. b	2. c	
3. e	16. d	3. a	3. b	3. d	3. b	
4. c	17. b	4. c	4. b	4. b	4. c	
5. d	18. d	5. c	5. b	5. c	5. a	
6. c	19. b	6. b	6. d	6. d	6. b	
7. a	20. c	7. d	7. a	7. c	7. b	
8. b	21. a	8. b	8. a	8. b	8. c	
9. d	22. f	9. c	9. d	9. b	9. a	
10. b		10. a	10. b	10. d		
11. c		11. a	11. c			
12. a		12. c				
13. b		13				

Chapters 13,14	Chapters 15,16	Chapters 17,18	Chapters 19,20
1. c	1. b	1. d	1. d
2. d	2. d	2. b	2. c
3. b	3. a	3. a	3. d
4. d	4. c	4. d	4. b
5. b	5. d	5. c	5. c
6. a	6. a	6. a	6. b
7. c	7. a	7. b	7. a
	8. c	8. c	8. d

PREREADING VOCABULARY WORKSHEETS

Vocabulary - *Jacob Have I Loved*

Rass Island, Chapters 1 and 2   Part I: Using Prior Knowledge and Contextual Clues
Below are the sentences in which the vocabulary words appear in the text. Read the sentence. Use any clues you can find in the sentence combined with your prior knowledge, and write what you think the underlined words mean in the space provided.

1. I chose the spot with care, for cordgrass alone is rough enough to rip the skin, and ours often concealed a bit of curling tin or <u>shards</u> of glass or crockery or jagged shells not yet worn thin by the tides

2. The ferry will be almost there before I can see Rass, lying low as a <u>terrapin</u> back on the faded olive water of the Chesapeake.

3. At thirteen I was tall and large boned, with <u>delusions</u> of beauty and romance.

4. Call jerked his head around to give me one of his looks, but the washboards of a skiff are a <u>precarious</u> perch at best, so he didn't stare long enough to waste time or risk a dunking.

5. I smiled at my sister <u>benevolently.</u>

6. My grandmother always complained that no good Methodist would put spirits into food. But my mother was <u>undaunted.</u>

7. If my father had not gone to France in 1918 and collected a hip full of <u>shrapnel</u>, Caroline and I would never have been born.

8. How the midwife smacked and prayed and <u>cajoled</u> the tiny chest to move.

9. Within a few weeks it was <u>lugubriously</u> out of tune.

10. I was proud of my sister, but that year something began to <u>rankle</u> beneath the pride.

Vocabulary - *Jacob Have I Loved* Chapters 1 and 2 Continued

Part II: Determining the Meaning   Match the words to their dictionary definitions.

___ 1. shards   A dangerously insecure; unstable
___ 2. terrapin   B. irritate or cause resentment
___ 3. delusions   C. mournfully; gloomily
___ 4. precarious   D. kindly
___ 5. benevolently   E. urged; appealed
___ 6. undaunted   F. fragments of a brittle substance, as of glass or metal
___ 7. shrapnel   G. false beliefs or opinions
___ 8. cajoled   H. not discouraged or disheartened
___ 9. lugubriously   I. North American aquatic turtle
___10. rankle   J. shell fragments from an explosion

Vocabulary - *Jacob Have I Loved* Chapters 3 and 4

Part I: Using Prior Knowledge and Contextual Clues
Below are the sentences in which the vocabulary words appear in the text. Read the sentence. Use any clues you can find in the sentence combined with your prior knowledge, and write what you think the underlined words mean in the space provided.

1. The machinations of European powers and the funny little mustached German dictator were as remote to our island in the fall of 1941 as Silas Marner, which sapped our energies through eighth-grade English.

2. There was no remonstrance for having broken the Fourth Commandment.

3. At six, Grandma woke, hungry and petulant.

4. In chorus one morning the irony of celebrating the birth of the Prince of Peace suddenly seemed too much .

5. Old Joshua's stamp remained on upon us- Sunday school and Sunday service morning and evening, and on Wednesday night prayer meeting where the more fervent would stand witness to the Lord's mercies of the preceding week and all the straying would be held up in prayer before the throne of Grace.

6. He was clearly discomfited by my behavior.

7. It was almost perfect, just a fraction flatter and shakier than Betty Jean's voice had been, the o's and ah's parodies of Betty Jean's pretentious ones

8. "Call me no longer Wheeze, but Sara Louise," I said grandly, smiling in the darkness, casting off the nickname she had diminished me with since we were two.

9. I had seldom felt so exasperated- to have to go home in the middle of this unfolding drama.

10. I began to read the verses on the tombstones with a certain pleasant melancholy.

Vocabulary - *Jacob Have I Loved* Chapters 3 and 4 Continued

Part II: Determining the Meaning   Match the words to their dictionary definitions.

___ 11. machinations   A. sadness
___ 12. remonstrance   B. angered or annoyed greatly
___ 13. petulant   C. having or showing great emotion or zeal; ardent
___ 14. irony   D. objection; protest
___ 15. fervent   E. schemes; plots
___ 16. discomfited   F. puffed-up; self-important
___ 17. pretentious   G. irritable or ill-tempered; peevish
___ 18. diminished   H. made smaller; lessened
___ 19. exasperated   I. contrast; incongruity
___ 20. melancholy   J. frustrated

Vocabulary - *Jacob Have I Loved* Chapters 5 and 6

Part I: Using Prior Knowledge and Contextual Clues
Below are the sentences in which the vocabulary words appear in the text. Read the sentence. Use any clues you can find in the sentence combined with your prior knowledge, and write what you think the underlined words mean in the space provided.

1. When it became apparent that the mast had been chopped down, rather than felled by lightning, Hiram Wallace became the butt of all the watermen's jokes.

2. After the storm passed, they were sighted drifting mastless on the Bay and were towed home by an obliging neighbor.

3. Some of the islanders thought a delegation should be sent to ask the old man straight out who he was, for if he were not Hiram Wallace, what right did he have taking over the Wallace property?

4. "It sounds like a vaudeville act."

5. Even as I yelled, I could feel a tiny rivulet of satisfaction invading the flood of my anger.

6. Without a word, she would turn and leave me before I was through, shutting off my torrent, so that my feelings, thus dammed, raged on in my chest.

7. Always there were two feelings in the dream - a wild exultation that now I was free of her and. . . .terrible guilt.

8. Crabs are fickle creatures.

9. I fancied myself the perfect lyricist - romantic, yet knowledgeable.

10. If he was not a spy, if he was indeed Hiram Wallace, why had he come back after all these years to an island where he was hardly remembered except with contempt?

Vocabulary - *Jacob Have I Loved* Chapters 5 and 6 Continued

Part II: Determining the Meaning   Match the words to their dictionary definitions.

___ 21. felled   A. song writer
___ 23. delegation   B. great joy
___ 22. obliging   C. changeable
___ 24. vaudeville   D. stage act
___ 25. rivulet   E. chopped
___ 26. torrent   F. assigned group
___ 27. exultation   G. flood; overflow
___ 28. fickle   H. helpful
___ 29. lyricist   I. hatred
___ 30. contempt   J. small stream

Vocabulary - *Jacob Have I Loved* Chapters 7, 8, and 9

Part I: Using Prior Knowledge and Contextual Clues
Below are the sentences in which the vocabulary words appear in the text. Read the sentence. Use any clues you can find in the sentence combined with your prior knowledge, and write what you think the underlined words mean in the space provided.

1. I don't mind admitting I wasn't too keen to step out on that ramshackle dock, but after Call had jumped onto it, and it had only shuddered a bit, I climbed carefully out and walked off to shore as quickly as I dared.

2. He took another futile swing before he answered.

3. That was far more wonderful than being a saboteur to be caught or an imposter to be exposed.

4. If I let go the tom to knock or open the door, I might lose him, so I just stood there on the dilapidated porch and hollered.

5. But despite these aberrations he seemed to be accepted as an islander, simply because he had called Auntie Braxton "Trudy," a name nobody had used for her since she was a young woman.

6. The Captain made both me and Call sit down in his clean, refurbished living room.

7. Very gingerly we loaded the live sacks onto it.

8. Just then, a piteous little cry rose from the sack nearest my feet.

9. "Tame them?" I snorted. "How, Caroline?" Call was definitely interested. "Paregoric," she said.

10. They laughed and imitated the befuddled women at the door.

Vocabulary - *Jacob Have I Loved* Chapters 7 and 8

Part II: Determining the Meaning   Match the words to their dictionary definitions.

___ 31. ramshackle   A. shabby; neglected
___ 32. futile   B. puzzled; perplexed
___ 33. saboteur   C. carefully
___ 34. dilapidated   D. hopeless
___ 35. aberrations   E. refinished
___ 36. refurbished   F. pitiful; pathetic
___ 37. gingerly   G. one who commits sabotage
___ 38. piteous   H. falling to ruin; tumble-down
___ 39. paregoric   I. opium form taken to relieve intestinal pain
___ 40. befuddled   J. quirks; abnormalities

Vocabulary - *Jacob Have I Loved* Chapters 10, 11, and 12

Part I: Using Prior Knowledge and Contextual Clues
Below are the sentences in which the vocabulary words appear in the text. Read the sentence. Use any clues you can find in the sentence combined with your prior knowledge, and write what you think the underlined words mean in the space provided.

1. My father, like any true waterman, could smell the storm coming up, even before the ominous rust-colored sunset.

2. Even with his stocky waterman's body to break the wind, our journey back up the path was a treacherous one.

3. "Best douse the lamp, Susan," my father said.

4. Grandma stopped her litany.

5. For while our noses and lungs feasted on nature's goodness, our eyes were assaulted by evidence of her savagery.

6. My reverie was punctured by a raucous cackling and complaining from a tiny house floating past us.

7. The storm had been capricious.

8. "Whosoever shall say, 'Thou fool,' shall be in danger of hell fire'" she quoted piously.

9. On the other hand, there was a certain safety in the unrelenting boredom of each day.

10. It was a ritual, as serious as the morning prayers of a missionary, and one which I took pains to finish well before Caroline could be expected to wake up.

11. "T'ain't fitting a heathen should read the Word of God," she said.

Vocabulary - *Jacob Have I Loved* Chapters 10-12

Part II: Determining the Meaning Match the words to their dictionary definitions.

___ 41. ominous
___ 42. treacherous
___ 43. douse
___ 44. litany
___ 45. savagery
___ 46. reverie
___ 47. capricious
___ 48. piously
___ 49. unrelenting
___ 50. ritual
___ 51. heathen

A. custom
B. extremely unsafe
C. put out; extinguish
D. cruelty
E. never changing; strict
F. devoutly; religiously
G. erratic; unpredictable
H. series of prayers
I. dream
J. threatening
K. unbeliever, pagan

Vocabulary - *Jacob Have I Loved* Chapters 13 and 14

Part I: Using Prior Knowledge and Contextual Clues
Below are the sentences in which the vocabulary words appear in the text. Read the sentence. Use any clues you can find in the sentence combined with your prior knowledge, and write what you think the underlined words mean in the space provided.

1. But my grandmother was adamant. "I'll not have that heathen in my house, much less in my bed."

2. It was up to Call to stop her. He would. I was sure- he and his tight little sense of propriety.

3. I suppose it is to Caroline's credit that she seldom sulked about this deprivation.

4. I pretended to study a torn cuticle to miss his scrutiny.

5. I propped my forehead on my elbowed hand and steeled myself for the cackle from Auntie Braxton and the laugh, which reminded me of an exuberant tuba, that would come from the Captain.

6. His mother and grandmother were destitute, and my father offered to take him aboard the *Portia Sue* as an oyster culler.

7. He was invited perfunctorily every Sunday, but he seemed to know that he oughn't to come and always managed an excuse.

8. You see, Trudy left a little legacy.

Part II: Determining the Meaning Match the words to their dictionary definitions.
___ 52. adamant   A. inheritance; sum of money
___ 53. propriety   B. loss
___ 54. deprivation   C. rightness
___ 55. scrutiny   D. examination; close attention
___ 56. exuberant   E. loud; cheerful
___ 57. destitute   F. routinely; impersonally
___ 58. perfunctorily   G. immovable; rigid
___ 59. legacy   H. very poor

Vocabulary - *Jacob Have I Loved* Chapters 15 and 16

Part I: Using Prior Knowledge and Contextual Clues

    Below are the sentences in which the vocabulary words appear in the text. Read the sentence. Use any clues you can find in the sentence combined with your prior knowledge, and write what you think the underlined words mean.

1. It was her <u>conniving</u> that helped Jacob steal the blessing from his brother.

2. She was trying to get rid of me. "Crisfield!" I cried <u>contemptuously</u>. "I'd rather be chopped for crab bait!"

3. I suppose if I were to try to stick a pin through that most <u>elusive</u> spot "the happiest days of my life," that strange winter on the *Portia Sue* with my father would have to be indicated.

4. <u>Censorship</u> kept Call from revealing much about where he was or what was going on, but in what he didn't say there was enough to make my skin crawl.

5. My grandmother, catching somehow the ultimate terror that the bomb promised, turned from adultery to <u>Armageddon</u>.

6. "It's good to be back," Call said, covering the old man's <u>discomposure</u>.

7. They were exchanging <u>inanities</u> about the size and terrors of New York, but my body knew that the conversation was about something far more threatening.

8. As it was, I <u>extricated</u> myself as quickly as I could from them and made my way, not home, but back to the crab house where I proceeded to ruin my only decent dress fishing the floats.

Part II: Determining the Meaning   Match the words to their dictionary definitions.

___ 60. conniving   A. removal of wartime info; deletion
___ 61. contemptuously   B. removed
___ 62. elusive   C. awkwardness
___ 63. censorship   D. scheming
___ 64. Armageddon   E. small talk
___ 65. discomposure   F. hard to pin down; slippery
___ 66. inanities   G. final battle between evil and good; end of the world
___ 67. extricated   H. defiantly; wildly

Vocabulary - *Jacob Have I Loved* Chapters 17 and 18

Part I: Using Prior Knowledge and Contextual Clues
Below are the sentences in which the vocabulary words appear in the text. Read the sentence. Use any clues you can find in the sentence combined with your prior knowledge, and write what you think the underlined words mean in the space provided.

1. "It's so good to be old," he said. "Youth is a mortal wound."

2. First, a kind of perverted pride that my meek mother had bested the old woman.

3. My mother murmured her reply without risking further rancor.

4. "Don't know?" It was almost a taunt. I was fidgeting under his gaze.

5. "It is better, "I recited piously, " 'to live in a corner of the housetop than in a house with a contentious woman.' "

6. "I wanted to get away from what I thought of as a very conventional small town and try my wings."

7. She added the last as though it explained her renunciation of Paris.

8. The question was coated with sarcasm.

Part II: Determining the Meaning Match the words to their dictionary definitions.

___ 68. mortal   A. average; traditional
___ 69. perverted   B. quarrelsome
___ 70. rancor   C. abandonment; denial
___ 71. taunt   D. bitter, long-lasting resentment
___ 72. contentious   E. fatal; deadly
___ 73. conventional   F. distorted; misguided
___ 74. renunciation   G. mock or jeer
___ 75. sarcasm   H. cutting remark intended to wound

61

Vocabulary - *Jacob Have I Loved* Chapters 19 and 20

Part I: Using Prior Knowledge and Contextual Clues
Below are the sentences in which the vocabulary words appear in the text. Read the sentence. Use any clues you can find in the sentence combined with your prior knowledge, and write what you think the underlined words mean in the space provided.

1. The truth, of course, is that the ailment crosses <u>denominational</u> lines.

2. Most of them only see the ungiving soil from which a man must wrestle his <u>subsistence</u> and the barriers that shut him out from the world.

3. It was a crisp, blue day that made me feel as I walked across the <u>quadrangle</u> that out near Rass the crabs were beginning to move.

4. He was already learning <u>midwifery</u>, and I think my mother understood that he would have been disappointed not to deliver our child himself.

5. I suppose every mother is reduced to <u>idiocy</u> when describing her firstborn, but, oh, he is a beauty.

Part II: Determining the Meaning   Match the words to their dictionary definitions.

___ 76. denominational   A. extreme foolishness
___ 77. subsistence   B. meager existence
___ 78. quadrangle   C. religious grouping
___ 79. midwifery   D. courtyard enclosed by buildings
___ 80. idiocy   E. practices of women who deliver babies

ANSWER KEY: VOCABULARY *Jacob Have I Loved*

Rass Island

Chapters 1,2
1. F
2. I
3. G
4. A
5. D
6. H
7. J
8. E
9. C
10. B

Chapters 3,4
11. E
12. D
13. G
14. I
15. C
16. J
17. F
18. H
19. B
20. A

Chapters 5,6
21. E
22. H
23. F
24. D
25. J
26. G
27. C
28. B
29. A
30. I

Chapters 7-9
31. H
32. D
33. G
34. A
35. J
36. E
37. C
38. F
39. I
40. B

Chapters 10-12
41. J
42. B
43. C
44. H
45. D
46. I
47. G
48. F
49. E
50. A
51. K

Chapters 13,14
52. G
53. C
54. B
55. D
56. E
57. H
58. F
59. A

Chapters 15,16
60. D
61. H
62. F
63. A
64. G
65. C
66. E
67. B

Chapters 17,18
68. E
69. F
70. D
71. G
72. B
73. A
74. C
75. H

Chapters 19,20
76. C
77. B
78. D
79. E
80. A

DAILY LESSONS

LESSON ONE

Objectives
1. To give students background information for *Jacob Have I Loved*
2. To give students the opportunity to fulfill their nonfiction reading assignment that goes along with this unit
3. To give students practice using library resources
4. To prepare students for the introductory activity in Lesson Two.
5. To give students the opportunity to write to inform by developing and organizing facts to convey information.

Activity

Assign one of each of the following topics to each of your students. Distribute Writing Assignment #1. Discuss the directions in detail. Take your students to the library so they may work on the assignment. Students should fill out a "Nonfiction Assignment Sheet" for at least one of the sources they used, and students should submit these sheets with their compositions.

Topics
1. Where is Pearl Harbor and what did it have to do with the U. S.'s entry into World War II?
2. Make a timeline of World War II.
3. Who were the Allies and name their leaders?
4. Name the Axis countries and their leaders.
5. Write a short biography of Franklin D. Roosevelt.
6. Identify the various theatres (areas) of fighting during World War II.
7. Identify Adolf Hitler and his role in the Third Reich.
8. Explain what a Nazi was.
9. What was "D- Day"?
10. What was "V-E Day"?
11. What was "V-J Day"?
12. Where is Hiroshima and what happened there?
13. Define patriotism. Why is it at a high point during a war?
14. What is meant by the home front?
15. Who was Rosie the Riveter?
16. What was rationing and why was it needed during this time period?
17. How did youngsters contribute to the war effort?
18. What were war bonds?
19. What was censorship and why was it necessary?
20. Identify popular songs, bands, and music of the era.
21. Why were radios, newspapers, and magazines so important back then?
22. What were black out curtains and why were they needed?

23. What were "victory gardens" and who had them?
24. Define sabotage and give examples of its use in World War II.
25. Tell what a U-boat is and its use.
26. Answer this question after reading something on national defense of the time period. Would you have been safer living inland or living on one of the coasts of the U.S. during the 1940's?
27. Locate the Chesapeake Bay area and determine how its occupants earned a living in the 1940's.
28. What is it like to be a twin?
29. Describe the life of a waterman on the bay, past and or present.
30. Learn about the market for crabs and seafood. What are some recipes for crab and other seafood found in the bay?

WRITING ASSIGNMENT #1 *Jacob Have I Loved*

PROMPT

You are going to read about Sara Louise Bradshaw and her twin sister, Caroline, 13 year-old fraternal twins who live on an isolated island in the Chesapeake Bay during World War II. It is realistic or historical fiction (the events in the novel *could* have taken place, but the characters and events are *fictional*). Before you read it, however, you should have some background information about some of the things mentioned in the story.

You have been assigned one topic about which you must find information. You are to read as much as you can about that topic and write a composition in which you relate what you have learned from your reading. Note that this is a *composition*, not just a sentence or two.

PREWRITING

You will go to the library. When you get there, use the library's resources to find information about your topic. Look for books, encyclopedias, articles in magazines- anything that will give you the information you require. Take a few notes as you read to help you remember important dates, names, places, or other details that will be important in your composition. After you have gathered information and become well-read on the subject of your report, make a little outline, putting your facts in order.

DRAFTING

You will need an introductory paragraph in which you introduce your topic.

In the body of your composition, put the "meat" of your research- the facts you found- in paragraph form. Each paragraph should have a topic sentence (a sentence letting the reader know what the paragraph will be about) followed by an explanation, examples or details.

Write a concluding paragraph in which you summarize the information you found and conclude your report.

PROMPT

After you have finished a rough draft of your paper, revise it yourself until you are happy with your work. Then, ask a student who sits near you to tell you what he/she likes best about your work, and what things he/she thinks can be improved. Take another look at your composition, keeping in mind your critic's suggestions, and make the revisions you feel are necessary.

PROOFREADING

Do a final proofreading of your paper double-checking your grammar, spelling, organization, and the clarity of your ideas.

NONFICTION ASSIGNMENT SHEET *Jacob Have I Loved*
(To be completed after reading the required nonfiction article)

Name _____ Date _____

Title of Nonfiction Read _____

Written By _____ Publication Date _____

I. Factual Summary: Write a short summary of the piece you read.

II. Vocabulary
    1. With which vocabulary words in the piece did you encounter some degree of difficulty?

    2. How did you resolve your lack of understanding with these words?

III. Interpretation: What was the main point the author wanted you to get from reading his work?

IV. Criticism
    1. With which points of the piece did you agree or find easy to accept? Why?

    2. With which points of the piece did you disagree or find difficult to believe? Why?

V. Personal Response: What do you think about this piece? OR How does this piece influence your ideas?

LESSON TWO

Objectives
1. To introduce The *Jacob Have I Loved* unit
2. To distribute books and other related materials
3. To check students' nonfiction reading assignments
4. To model effective oral reading skills by reading the introduction, Rass Island, aloud
5. To have students identify the setting, point of view, and the author's use of flashback as a literary device.

Note: Prior to this class period, please put up a bulletin board titled: WORLD WAR II, AN ISLAND VIEW (or some other appropriate title). If you do not have a bulletin board to use, use a big sheet of paper put over the chalkboard or a flip-chart style paper on an easel. Be sure to include an outline of a world map. Have a separate map of the Chesapeake Bay displayed. You may want to **not** include the locations, and allow students to figure these out as the novel goes on.

Activity #1
Provide students with a plain file card, posterboard strip, or something similar. Have each of them write one fact he/she learned from his/her research. Students could briefly illustrate their fact card if time allows. Then have students place their fact card on the bulletin board. If it has to do with location (i.e. South Pacific, Chesapeake Bay, etc.) guide students into a correct placement. So vital locations aren't covered up, students could use yarn to point to location and place card to the side. Encourage placement for an attractive display. Students could also write directly on the bulletin board paper. Discuss each fact briefly as it is presented so all students will be exposed to a wide variety of background information before reading.

TRANSITION: One or more students will have placed a fact near the setting of the novel. Question them to determine their prior knowledge about this location. Fill in unknown basics (such as: isolated island, Chesapeake Bay, estuary, watershed) and ask them what they think life would be like for a pair of twins their age living there during World War II. They will soon find out!

Activity #2
Distribute the materials students will use in this unit. Explain in detail how students are to use these materials.

Study Guides Students should preview the study guide questions before each reading assignment to get a feeling for what events and ideas are important in that section. After reading the section, students will (as a class or individually) answer the questions to review the important events and ideas from that section of the book. Students should keep the study guides as study materials for the unit test.

Vocabulary   Prior to reading a reading assignment, students will do vocabulary work related to the section of the book they are about to read. Following the completion of the reading of the book, there will be a vocabulary review of all the words used in the vocabulary assignments. Students should keep their vocabulary work as study materials for the unit test.

Reading Assignment Sheet   You need to fill in the reading assignment sheet to let students know when their reading has to be completed. You can either write the assignment sheet on a side blackboard or bulletin board and leave it there for students to see each day, or you can "ditto" copies for each student to have. In either case, you should advise students to become very familiar with the reading assignments so they know what is expected of them.

Extra Activities Center   The Unit Resource portion of this unit contains suggestions for a library of related books and articles in your classroom as well as crossword and word search puzzles. Make an extra activities center in your room where you will keep these materials for students to use. (Bring the books and articles in from the library and keep several copies of the puzzles on hand.) Explain to students that these materials are available for students to use when they finish reading assignments or other class work early

Books   Each school has its own rules and regulations regarding student use of school books. Advise students of the procedures that are normal for your school.

Activity #3

Have students examine cover of book and turn to introduction, Rass Island. Read these four pages to them as they follow along. Identify from whose point of view the story is being told, relish in the vivid descriptions of setting, and accept the author's use of flashback. If time permits, try to have them answer Study Guide Questions about Rass Island (?s1-3) from first set (Rass Island, Ch.1,2). Assign P,V,R for (Preview Study Questions, Vocabulary Work and Read) Chapters 1 and 2.

LESSON THREE

Objectives
1. To review the main events and ideas from Rass Island and chapters 1 and 2
2. To preview the study questions for chapters 3 and 4
3. To familiarize students with the vocabulary in chapters 3 and 4
4. To begin the reading of chapter 3

Activity #1

Discuss the answers to the study questions for Rass Island and chapters 1 and 2 in detail. Write the answers on the board or overhead transparency so students can have the correct answers for study purposes. Note: It is a good practice in public speaking and leadership skills for individual students to take charge of leading the discussions of the study questions. Perhaps a different student could go to the front of the class and lead the discussion each day that the study questions are discussed during this unit. Of course, the teacher should guide the discussion when appropriate and be sure to fill in any gaps the students leave.

Activity #2

Give students the remaining class time to preview the study questions for chapters 3 and 4 of *Jacob Have I Loved* and to do the related vocabulary work. If time allows, begin reading chapter 3 or assign the reading of chapters 3 and 4 to be completed prior to the next class session.

LESSON FOUR

Objectives
1. To review the main events and ideas from chapters 3 and 4
2. To familiarize students with vocabulary from chapters 5 and 6
3. To preview study questions for chapters 5 and 6

Activity #1

Discuss the answers to the study questions for chapters 3 and 4 as you have done the study questions previously.

Activity #2

Have students look over the prereading vocabulary work for chapters 5 and 6 for about 10 minutes. Use the matching section of the vocabulary pages as a springboard for a game similar to concentration. Divide students into groups of four or five. Have students quickly copy the vocabulary words (divide the task into sections to expedite) and their clues on separate index cards. Turn them all over. Have students in their small groups take turns flipping over two of the cards. If they are a match, i.e. a vocabulary word matches with its meaning, they keep the pair and get another turn. Students may look at the vocabulary words in their sentences for contextual clues. Continue play until all cards are matched into sets.

Activity #3

Give students any remaining time to look over study questions for chapters 5 and 6. Assign reading of these two chapters to be done prior to the next class session.

NOTE: Explain to students that you will be having writing conferences in the next class session. During the writing conference, you will discuss their writing skills individually, based on their first writing assignment in this unit (World War II information).

LESSON FIVE

Objectives
1. To review the main events and ideas of chapters 5 and 6
2. To evaluate students' writing
3. To have students revise their Writing Assignment 1 papers

Activity #1

Use the multiple choice format of the study guide questions for chapters 5 and 6 as a quiz to check that students have done the required reading and to review the main ideas of chapters 5 and 6. Exchange papers for checking. Discuss answers and make sure students take notes for studying purposes.

Activity #2

Assign the prereading vocabulary pages, study guide questions and reading of chapters 7, 8, and 9. Students should work on this while they are waiting for their conference with you.

Activity #3

Call students to your desk (or some other private area) to discuss their papers from Writing Assignment 1. Use the following Writing Evaluation Form to help structure your conference. Give students a date when their revisions are due.

WRITING EVALUATION FORM - *Jacob Have I Loved*

Name _____ Date _____

Writing Assignment #1 for the *Jacob Have I Loved* unit   Grade _____

Circle One For Each Item:

Description (paragraph 1)	excellent	good	fair	poor
Plans (body paragraphs)	excellent	workable	fair	not realistic
Conclusion	excellent	good	fair	poor
Grammar:	excellent	good	fair	poor (errors noted)
Spelling:	excellent	good	fair	poor (errors noted)
Punctuation:	excellent	good	fair	poor (errors noted)
Legibility:	excellent	good	fair	poor

Strengths:

Weaknesses:

Comments/Suggestions:

LESSON SIX

Objectives
1. To review the main ideas of chapters 7, 8, and 9
2. To do the prereading vocabulary work for chapters 10, 11, and 12
3. To preview the study questions for chapters 10, 11, and 12
4. To expose figurative language to students

Activity #1
Hand out four little slips of paper or mini cards to each student that have the letters A, B, C, or D on them. A good idea is to use different color cards for each letter. Use the multiple choice study guide questions and answers on Chapters 7, 8, and 9 for an oral review. Read the question (and/ or show it on the overhead). Then give students the four possible answers, labeling them A, B, C, or D (or show on overhead again). Students respond by holding up the card with what they think is the correct answer. This is one variety of Every Student Response. Remind students not to look at what others are holding up, but to simply display the card of their choice. This is a quick indicator of students' comprehension. You can make it somewhat different by requiring complete silence and having them read the questions silently from the overhead, or make it more mysterious (fun?) by blindfolding everyone and have them hold up a certain number of fingers per answer instead of using the cards.

Activity #2
Have students pair up and do the prereading work together for chapters 10, 11, and 12.

Activity #3
Give students remaining time to review chapters 10-12 study guide questions, and possibly begin their reading of chapters 10-12. Inform them that the reading from these chapters is due in **two** class lessons.

Activity #4
Within the last 5-8 minutes of class, turn the class's attention to your reading of the following examples of figurative language from their upcoming reading (just ask them to listen):

- our noses and lungs feasted on nature's goodness
- shaken by a giant hand that scooped them up and flung them into the boiling sea
- wind grabbed this old house by the scruff of the neck and shook the bejeebers out
- the wind screaming like a giant wounded dove
- like any true waterman, could smell the storm
- I felt as I always did when someone told the story of my birth
- Why don't you just teach a crab to play the piano?
- dragged at me like a lead weight on a crab pot

Inquire if they see any similarities in these passages, or have any idea what these are examples of? Encourage them to do some research tonight if no one comes up with "figures of speech" (personification, etc.) or "figurative language." Tell them that in the next class session they will become very familiar with these and many more passages like them from their novel.

LESSON SEVEN

Objectives
1. To introduce simile, personification, and metaphor as figures of speech
2. To distinguish between three different types of figurative language
3. To have students locate figurative language in the text
4. To create original figures of speech
5. To illustrate figurative language

Activity #1

Review any of the previous introduction that was successful. If any students identified the passages correctly, continue allowing them to explain. If not, once again read some examples from the text and determine what makes them figurative language. Make three columns on the chalkboard labeling each one separately: simile, metaphor, and personification. Spend some time here instructing about these three forms of figurative language. Perhaps you could cite some examples from familar songs. Ask why they think any author or lyricist would use them? Do they use them? Why? In what way does using them enhance speaking or writing or the understanding of each of these. As a whole group, have students give you examples they can think of and then have them locate a few in any part of the text they have read. Allow them to come to the board and write these under the correct heading. When you are satisfied with their ability to recognize them go to the next activity.

Activity #2

Divide the class into small groups of three or four. Have each group assign a recorder. Give them a couple of sheets of paper. Ask each group to locate as many of these figures of speech as they can from the text. They may be more successful in the portion they already have read, but it isn't necessary to limit them. Giving them a time constraint is an option. It could be a race, you are the judge. Offer a special incentive for the group that can most quickly find the figurative language-rich beginning chapter page that has two similes, three personifications, and one metaphor. (chapter 8) You may want to rule out using the ones that are posted on the board. It's up to you. There are a wealth of them present in the text, they'll find plenty. Wrap this activity up by having the group with the **most** read their list aloud. Decide as a whole group if indeed each one is correct. Have all groups check off the ones that are read that they also found. Allow every group to read any that have not yet been mentioned. You could give small treats for first, second, third place, etc.

Activity #3
Have students create one example of each type. They could be individual sentences or you could require them to write a short paragraph using all three. Base this on the ability level of your students and/or time. Create one together as a model. If there is time, have them illustrate it with original art work or magazine pictures. Save finished products for display. They could do this part as homework.

NOTE: The following figurative language test is optional. You may want to use it right after instruction, later in unit, or not at all. You may choose to use it only as a resource for this lesson. It contains examples from the entire book.

FIGURATIVE LANGUAGE TEST

I. Read the following examples of figurative language. Label each one separately with either an **S** for simile, **P** for personification, or an **M** for metaphor. **BONUS**: Circle the 5 that are both an S and a P.

1. So as the water nibbled away at our land, the war nibbled away at our souls. _____
2. Shiny as a new crab pot, all set to capture the world. _____
3. I don't need watched like one of your old peelers. _____
4. August and February are both alike in one way. They're both dream killers. _____
5. I felt as though God had lowered a giant glass lid over the whole steaming Bay. _____
6. The three trees were still there, looking a bit like little boys after their summer haircuts. _____
7. Relief washed over me like a gentle surf. _____
8. It was like cuddling a stone. _____
9. Just the look on the Captain's face ripped my heart right out of my chest. _____
10. Call turned the color of a steamed crab at her touch. _____
11. For awhile our noses and lungs feasted on nature's goodness, our eyes were assaulted by evidence of her savagery. _____
12. Why don't you just teach a crab to play the piano? _____
13. It was hard to fight the wind screaming like a giant wounded dove. _____
14. February hits you right in the stomach. _____
15. I knew of course, I knew as though I were swallowing an icicle. _____
16. I had forgotten, that life, like a crab pot, catches a lot of trash you haven't bargained for. _____
17. As gently as she might coax a nocturne from our old piano. _____
18. I followed them to Auntie Braxton's house like a beaten hunting pup. _____
19. I sat there stunned, as though someone had thrown a rock in my face. _____
20. It was a ritual as serious as the morning prayers of a missionary. _____
21. Shaking her hand was like holding a bunch of twigs. _____
22. Anything dumber than a blowfish, it's a county board of education. _____
23. Youth is a mortal wound. _____
24. The old lady moaned like someone disturbed by a bad dream. _____
25. I turned on her like a red-bellied snake. _____

Jacob Figurative Language Test Page 2

26. I could almost imagine I was an Egyptian slave taking Pharaoh on a tour of the flooded Nile Delta. _____
27. I was a good oyster in those days. Not even the presence of a radiant, grown-up Caroline could get under my shell. _____
28. February is just plain malicious. It knows when your defenses are down. _____
29. My spiritual health was about on par with a person who's been dead three days. _____
30. I reached in and turned the twin so that she was delivered head first, but blue as death. _____

II. List one example of your own for each type of figurative language. They can be original or from your favorite songs.

III. **Brain Teaser:** Can you spot the metaphor that sums up the **theme** of this novel 'in a nutshell'?

ANSWER KEY: FIGURATIVE LANGUAGE TEST *Jacob Have I Loved*

I.
1. P,S
2. S
3. S
4. M
5. S,P
6. S
7. P
8. S
9. P
10. S
11. P
12. P
13. P,S
14. P
15. S
16. P
17. S,P
18. S
19. S
20. S
21. S
22. M
23. N
24. S
25. S
26. M
27. M
28. P
29. M
30. S

II. Answers will vary.

III. Youth is a mortal wound.

LESSON EIGHT

Objectives
1. To review main events and ideas in chapters 10, 11, and 12
2. To do the prereading vocabulary work for chapters 13 and 14
3. To preview study guide questions for chapters 13 and 14

Activity #1

Use the multiple choice study guide questions as a quiz to test students reading of assigned text and as a review of the main ideas. Exchange papers to check. Discuss the answers to insure understanding. Encourage note taking for their later study use.

Activity #2

Have students spend about 10 minutes completing the prereading vocabulary page. After they have done that, pair them up. Have one member of each pair "act" out one of the words, while the other one tries to guess the word. Do this until all of the vocabulary words have been covered at least once. This is similar to the game Charades.

Activity #3

Have students preview study guide questions independently for chapters 13 and 14 in the remaining class time.

LESSON NINE

Objectives
1. To give students practice in writing to persuade
2. To read chapters 13 and 14
2. To give students practice reading orally
3. To evaluate students' oral reading

Activity #1

Have students read chapters 13 and 14 orally in class. You probably know the best way to get readers within your class; pick students at random, ask for volunteers, have students who have just read select another student, assign numbers to students and spin a spinner, whatever works best for you. Complete the oral reading evaluation form that follows this lesson after listening to your students read.

Activity #2

Distribute Writing Assignment #3 and discuss directions in detail. If there is any remaining class time, have them begin work on this assignment. Otherwise, give students specifics on when assignment is due.

ORAL READING EVALUATION *Jacob Have I Loved*

Name _____ Class____ Date _____

SKILL	EXCELLENT	GOOD	AVERAGE	FAIR	POOR
Fluency	5	4	3	2	1
Clarity	5	4	3	2	1
Audibility	5	4	3	2	1
Pronunciation	5	4	3	2	1
_____	5	4	3	2	1
_____	5	4	3	2	1

Total _____ Grade _____

Comments:

WRITING ASSIGNMENT #2   *Jacob Have I Loved*

PROMPT

Now that you have finished reading chapter 14, you know that Captain Wallace uses his widow's legacy to send Wheeze's twin sister, Caroline, to music school in Baltimore. He even claims Sara Louise was responsible for giving him the idea. He does this because Caroline has not been able to pursue her voice lessons in Salisbury due to the hardships of the war, and he and Trudy greatly enjoyed and valued her singing. He feels indebted to their family for befriending him and suggesting the marriage, and wants to give something back.

In this writing assignment, pretend you are the ever-passed over, unmusically gifted Wheeze. Your object is to convince Captain Wallace that his judgment is not sound or equitable and that you rightfully deserve some share of, if not all, the generosity and recognition he solely bestows on your musically gifted twin sister.

PREWRITING

To begin with, decide why you are so upset with the Captain's decision. On a piece of paper, list all the reasons why you disagree with his choice. Decide which are your strongest justifiable arguments, and which are less substantial. Organize your points from weaker to strongest and jot down anything you can think of which will support or explain your arguments.

DRAFTING

Begin with an introductory paragraph in which you express your outrage to the Captain for using Trudy's legacy to send Caroline to music school in Baltimore. Follow that with one paragraph for each of the main points you have to support your side of this argument. Fill in each paragraph with examples, facts, and feelings that support your main point. Then, write an ending paragraph in which you summarize your arguments and restate your discontent with the Captain as your final statement.

PROMPT

When you finish the rough draft of your paper, ask a student who sits near you to read it. After reading your rough draft, he\she should tell you what he\she liked best about your work, which parts were difficult to understand, and ways in which your work could be improved. Reread your paper considering your critic's comments, and make the corrections you think are necessary.

PROOFREADING

Do a final proofreading of your paper double-checking your grammar, spelling, organization, and the clarity of your ideas.

LESSON TEN

Objectives
1. To reveiw main events and ideas from chapters 13 and 14
2. To do the prereading vocabulary work for chapters 15 and 16
3. To preview study guide questions for chapters 15 and 16

Activity #1
Discuss the answers to the Study Guide Questions for chapters 13 and 14.

Activity #2
Have students spend approximately 10 minutes completing the prereading vocabulary work independently. Pass out plain paper for drawing, or use individual easels or slates. Have one of the partners sketch their impression of one of the vocabulary words within a limited amount of time. The other one is to guess which vocabulary word he/she is trying to picture. When the correct word has been chosen, play turns to the other partner. Continue play until all vocabulary has been covered for chapters 15 and 16. This is similar to the game Pictionary. It could also be done in small groups.

Activity #3
Assign previewing of Study Guide Questions and reading to be completed by next class.

LESSON ELEVEN

Objectives
1. To discuss PROJECT SAVE THE BAY, a project that goes along with this unit
2. Review the main events and ideas in chapters 15 and 16
3. To preview the prereading vocabulary work for chapters 17 and 18
4. To begin reading chapters 17 and 18

Activity #1

If you have decided to do Project Save the Bay with your students during this unit (instead of after it), take time now to explain what the project is and how the students will accomplish it. (See the information following this lesson for guidelines.)

Activity #2

Have students select the manner in which they would like to review the study guide questions for chapters 15 and 16. They could use any one of the previous tried activities, or encourage them to come up with one of their own.

Activity #3

Have students preview prereading vocabulary work independently and then begin reading chapters 17 and 18 silently. Remind them that the reading of these two chapters is due by the next class meeting.

PROJECT SAVE THE BAY

Objectives:
    Project Save the Bay is a total class project for use in conjunction with this novel. Since this entire novel revolves around the Bay and the watermen's dependence upon it, it seems an ideal occasion to make students aware of the environmental issues facing us all concerning water pollution and conservation. This novel and project can be taught at any time during the calendar year, although trying to tie it into an Earth Day (April) celebration may create an even more enthusiastic response from your students and community. It could also double for service learning project hours, if your school system has such a program. This project is intended to allow students the opportunity to actually do something concrete to contribute to environmental conservation. **Reminder:** These activities are universal and can be applied to any geographic area, not just the six states (New York, Pennsylvania, West Virginia, Virginia, Delaware, and Maryland) that comprise the Chesapeake Bay watershed (drainage basin). Wherever you see the **Bay** stated, just substitute your watershed area.

THE PROJECT
    This project is separate from the rest of the *Jacob Have I Loved* unit, so you can either use it while you are doing the *Jacob* unit or as a separate mini-unit after you have completed the unit test for the book. Also, having it as a separate project enables you to eliminate it if you want to or need to for some reason, without disrupting the normal flow of the unit.

    Assignment 1 Invite a speaker from a local agency (Chesapeake Bay Foundation, Department of Environmental Resources, etc.) to come to your class and do a presentation primarily on the problems facing the Bay. Many areas now have agencies exclusively devoted to conservation issues. If you are unable to secure someone outside of your school, perhaps a science teacher could address your class, or you could do one yourself, renting or borrowing videos or films. Be sure your students are adequately prepared for this presentation by: reviewing proper listening and questioning etiquette, and having them prepare a list of appropriate questions the night before.

    Assignment 2 Instead of you handling the previous mentioned activity, you could have your students research this topic and come up with appropriate and available resources and agencies to contact. They could then write letters of request to one or more of these places, requesting personnel come to their class to do a presentation. Follow up with a phone call to make specific arrangements.

    Assignment 3 After they have been exposed to the environmental issues facing the Bay, send them to the library to do some research. Each student should read and summarize at least two articles about preserving the environment of the Bay.

    Assignment 4 After students have done their research, have them give oral reports about the articles they have read so that all students are exposed to the wealth of information that has been collectively obtained. Try to keep a brief master summary of ideas on a large piece of newsprint as a class record.

Assignment 5 Divide students into groups of four or five. Explain that their job is to brainstorm specific ideas that they can individually, or as a group, actually do to assist in this conservation project. This can get as involved as you, the teacher, want. It could be as simple as creating posters listing conservation tips to post in local stores to projects involving your whole grade, school, or community. The more involved you make it, the more your students will learn if they are given the proper direction and opportunities. See what your students suggest.

The planning of these activities, whatever they may turn out to be, should be done in class. Breaking down your class into groups to handle different activities would be a good idea if you are involved in several activities. Each group needs to have various assigned roles to insure cooperative learning and completion of tasks. Discuss what is needed and assign accordingly. Many authentic-real life skills will be exercised and improved by your students during this type of follow-up. Be generous in your guidance and assistance, yet allow them to be decisive and responsible, as well. Plan how you will obtain materials and other required items as part of your group discussion.

Assignment 6 Have students carry out the plans they have decided upon. The types of activities they have come up with will determine the amount of class time needed. To foster accountability, schedule daily updates and reports on any out-of-class work. Students will need that check-up to maintain their enthusiasm and drive.

Assignment 7 When your Save the Bay activities are complete, take a day or two to evaluate the success of each project. Have the students create a checklist or form which measures the merits of each project. It could be filled out by each group, self-evaluating themselves, and/or by other groups, evaluating each other. Be sure you lead the students to include objective criteria, rather than subjective criteria which could lead to antagonism between groups. Also, have each student write their own personal evaluation, taking time to reflect back over their involvement in the project. You could also have them give themselves a grade based on their perception of what they deserve and why. If possible, briefly meet individually with students, or with their groups to discuss these evaluations with them. This may sound like an inordinate amount of time to devote to this project, but in the long run, it will be worth it for your students.

Assignment 8 Plan a field trip to the Bay. This will provide the most authentic culmination possible. You might choose a location such as a State Park, recreation area, or the ultimate visit would be to either Smith or Tangier Island. These are the islands that Rass was based upon. The author used watermen's experiences from these locations to develop her novel.
    For optimum real life student learning, this selection, once again could be done by the students, through their research and development. This activity could be a one day trip, or an extended length of time trip based on your resources and desires. How can your trip relate to your completed project? What you plan to do when you get here should be decided by your class with your direction. Check with your school system for guidelines governing off campus field trips. Parents are usually very willing to assist in chaperoning and planning these type excursions.

RESOURCES

The Alliance for the Chesapeake Bay
6600 York Road
Baltimore, MD 21212
(401) 377-6270
Fax (410) 377-7144

The Chesapeake Bay Foundation
162 Prince George Street
Annapolis, MD 21401
(301) 268-8816

The Chesapeake Bay Foundation
1001 E. Main Street, Suite 815
Richmond, VA 23219

The Chesapeake Bay Foundation
214 State Street
Harrisburg, PA 17101

Cruise Boat to Smith Island
The *Captain Tyler* departs Point Lookout (Scotland, MD) daily, Memorial Day-September. For information write to:
Captain Alan Tyler
 Rhodes Point, Maryland; 21858
Or call (301) 425- 2771

Cruise Boat to Tangier Island
The *Captain Thomas* sails from Reedville, May to mid-October. Reservations are necessary. Write to Tangier and ChesapeakeCruises, Inc., Box 36
Warsaw, Virginia 22572
or call (804) 891 2331.

Maryland Tourist Office
Dept. SL
45 Calvert Street
Annapolis, MD 21401
(301) 269- 3517

Virginia Division of Tourism
Dept. SL
202 North Ninth Street
Suite 500
Richmond, VA 23219
(804) 786-4484

LESSON TWELVE

Objectives
1. To review the main ideas, events, and quotations from chapters 17 and 18
2. To do the prereading vocabulary work for chapters 19 and 20
3. To preview the study guide questions for chapters 19 and 20

Activity #1

Have students pair up and quiz each other's comprehension using the study guide questions or the multiple choice format.

Activity #2

Allow each student to select another partner. Have them take turns reading quotes to each other to identify the speaker out of chapters 17 and 18. They could refer to other chapters as well. Encourage them to try to sound like the person whose quote it is by acting some out yourself and having them guess.

Activity #3

Have students independently do the prereading vocabulary work and preview the study guide questions for chapters 19 and 20.

LESSON THIRTEEN

Objectives
    1. To read chapters 19 and 20
    2. To answer study guide questions from chapters 19 and 20
    3. To locate geographical sites mentioned in the novel
    4. To characterize Truitt, Virginia

Activity #1

    Have students read chapters 19 and 20 orally, taking turns. Use earlier suggestions from Lesson 9 if you need some ideas.

Activity #2

    Have students answer study guide questions orally and discuss.

Activity # 3

    Place students in small groups. Have them list characteristics of Truitt, Virginia. While they are doing that, an artistic member of the group could sketch a brief outline of the community. Using the U.S. map, see if they can figure out where it would approximately be located based on the information given about distance from a hospital. Have them list other locales mentioned in the book and chart them on a map. (Crisfield, Smith Island, Salisbury, Baltimore, New York, Washington D.C., University of Maryland, University of Kentucky, etc.). What conclusions can be drawn (if any) based on the overall geographical locations mentioned?

LESSON FOURTEEN

Objectives
1. To give students the opportunity to practice writing to express personal ideas
2. To give students practice in preparing for and performing an interview
3. To draw attention to the importance of the twins' birth in this novel
4. To give the teacher the opportunity to evaluate students' narrative writing skills
5. To give students an opportunity to build relationships within their family

Activity

Distribute Writing Assignment #3 and discuss the directions in detail. Give students the remainder of class time to work on this assignment by preparing their questions. Tell them that they may share these accounts with the class at a later date. They may want to include memorabilia or pictures to enhance their presentation.

Note: Please be sensitive to any student who, for whatever reason, won't be able to (adoption, etc.) or care to (death, divorce, etc.) complete this assignment. Provide them with an alternative that still gives them practice writing a narrative to express personal ideas. Please handle this with discretion. Ideas: birth of a sibling or relative, an experience due to sharing room with a sibling, an experience resulting from sibling rivalry, etc.

LESSONS FIFTEEN AND SIXTEEN

Objectives
1. To discuss the ideas and themes from *Jacob Have I Loved* in greater detail
2. To have students exercise their interpretive and critical thinking skills
3. To try to relate some of the ideas in *Jacob Have I Loved* to the students' lives

Activity #1

Choose the questions from the Extra Discussion Questions/Writing Assignments which seem most appropriate for your students. A class discussion of these questions is most effective if students have been given the opportunity to formulate answers to the questions prior to the discussion. To this end, you may either have all the students formulate answers to all the questions, divide your class into groups and assign one or more questions to each group, or you could assign one question to each student in your class. The option you choose will make a difference in the amount of class time needed for this activity.

Activity #2

After students have had ample time to formulate answers to the questions, begin your class discussion of the questions and the ideas presented by the questions. Be sure students take notes during the discussion so they have information to study for the unit test.

WRITING ASSIGNMENT #3 *Jacob Have I Loved*

PROMPT

The story of Sara Louise and Caroline's birth is very important in this novel. The author even includes another birth of a set of twins at the conclusion of this novel.

Everyone seems to enjoy hearing or telling the story of their birth. Caroline intended to write her entire life story before she became famous. Most stories involve some of the same factors, and some may include unusual or unique circumstances. Interview your parents, your grandparents, your siblings, and/or any other interested party who can help you recreate the event that started you on your journey through life.

Your assignment is to recreate on paper, that very special time; the tale of your entry into the world. This will be a narrative piece of writing, retelling this memorable event that began your personal history.

PREWRITING

Before you actually interview anyone, create a list of questions that will help you obtain the information you need. After you have done that, it's time to start asking the questions. Interview as many people as necessary and feasible. Take notes on the information they give you. You may consider taping (audio) each one so you can refer back to the conversation, if needed. Be careful to keep your notes in a logical or chronological order.

DRAFTING

Begin your paper with an introductory paragraph giving your audience some background on yourself today. Include basic information about yourself: your name, your age, what you look like, your interests, etc. This paragraph's purpose is to lead into the body of your composition, which is coming next. The body of your composition should contain information you derived from your interviews. Using these specifics, start at some point of time (such as when your mother went into labor) and continue to tell the story, until you have completed that task. Be sure to include any interesting or humorous comments you recorded from your interviews. Be certain to use transition words to move your story along, such as: then, next, after, later on, at last, etc. Finish your composition with a concluding paragraph in which you express your opinion or make personal comment about this event.

PROOFREADING

When you finish your rough draft, ask a student who sits near you to read it. After reading your rough draft, he/she should tell you what he/she liked best about your work, which parts were difficult to understand, and ways in which your work could be improved. Reread your paper considering your critic's comments and make the corrections you think are necessary.

EXTRA DISCUSSION QUESTIONS/WRITING ASSIGNMENTS
Jacob Have I Loved

Interpretive

1. From whose point of view is this story told, and how does that influence the reader's perception of the story?

2. Identify the setting and tell how it dictates this story.

3. Are the characters in *Jacob Have I Loved* stereotypes? If so, explain the usefulness of employing stereotypes in the book. If they are not, explain how they merit individuality.

4. What are the main conflicts in the story, and how are they resolved?

5. What is foreshadowing? Give examples of foreshadowing used in *Jacob Have I Loved*.

6. Clarify flashback and explain its use in *Jacob Have I Loved*.

7. Give a complete character analysis of Sara Louise.

8. Formulate an accurate time line for the entire novel beginning with the summer of 1941. What information did you use to draw your conclusions?

9. Explain the role of each of these characters: Caroline, Call, Hiram Wallace, Grandma, Susan Bradshaw, Truitt Bradshaw, and Joseph Wojtkiewicz.

10. Define climax. Next, summarize the main events leading up to **it** and the remaining events after **it** that create the resolution.

11. Locate examples of the island dialect the characters use. How did its use influence your perception of the characters?

12. Wheeze uses but mispronounces the word, p-sychiatrist. What does this say about her?

Critical

13. Explain the significance of the title "*Jacob Have I Loved*."

14. We know from the author's use of flashback at the opening, that both Wheeze and Caroline leave the island. How does Katherine Paterson manage to hold our interest throughout the story up to the climax?

Jacob Have I Loved Extra Discussion Questions page 2

15. Compare and contrast the life of a Chesapeake Bay (or any other area) waterman today with his life in the 1940's.

16. Wheeze compares the men of Rass and Truitt in this way, " These men struggle against the mountains. On Rass men followed the water. There is a difference." What is she saying?

17. Why did Wheeze feel it was her responsibility to develop Call's sense of humor? How did she attempt to do this?

18. For what reason do you think Katherine Paterson has teen-aged Wheeze fall in love with seventy-year-old Captain Wallace?

19. Religious issues and Biblical references abound in this novel. Interpret the author's motivation for incorporating these ideas after reading a short biography of Katherine Paterson.

20. Who is responsible for Wheeze finally leaving the island? Defend your answer.

21. Describe Katherine Paterson's writing style, including her use of figurative language. How does it shape the reader's perception of the story?

22. Is the story of *Jacob Have I Loved* believable? Why or why not?

23. Essie's first-born twin, the healthy baby, was a boy. Do you think this was intentional on the author's part? Why or why not?

24. What universal themes are present in *Jacob Have I Loved*?

25. Why does Wheeze say, "I wonder if I shall ever feel as old as I did that Christmas with Grandma?"

26. How does Wheeze seem to come full circle by the end of the novel concerning her birth, her abilities, and her sister?

Jacob Have I Loved Extra Discussion Questions page 3

Critical/ Personal Response

27. Why did the islanders disapprove of Wheeze working the water with her father? Would people think differently today? Why or why not? Would you enjoy this sort of work? Explain.

28. When Wheeze is actually presented with an offer to go to boarding school in Crisfield, she furiously refuses. Why did she react in that manner when earlier that was her primary goal? Have you ever felt that sort of contradiction and behaved likewise? Explain.

29. Have you read any other books written by Katherine Paterson? How do they compare to *Jacob Have I Loved*? Which one is your favorite? Why?

30. Wheeze often has glorious dreams and daydreams where she is powerful and recognized. Cite some examples. Why do you think the author includes this element in Wheeze's characterization? Can you relate to this? Share some of your dreams.

31. While washing windows with her mother, Wheeze experiences a myriad of emotions ranging from pride, guilt, and anger, to fury. Do you think this is abnormal? Have you ever experienced this? Please share.

Personal Response

32. If you were Wheeze, what would you have done after the Captain gave Caroline the money for music school?

33. Suppose you are enrolled in college with high aspirations for a medical degree, like Wheeze. If your advisor tried to dash away your dream, such as Wheeze's did, what would you do?

34. What is the value of believing in yourself and developing your own special talents, despite the abilities and gifts of those near to you?

35. Will Wheeze make a 'good' mother? State your opinion and support it.

36. Would you have liked to live on Rass Island during World War II? Explain why or why not.

37. If you were Caroline, how would you have handled Wheeze's jealousy?

Jacob Have I Loved Extra Discussion Questions page 4

38. Do you or someone you know have an elderly grandparent living with them? If so, compare this situation to the Bradshaws. How do other family members cope?

39. How would you have tackled Auntie Braxton's cat problem?

40. Have you read any other historical fiction from this time period? If so, name them. In what ways were they similar to or different from *Jacob Have I Loved*?

41. Does sibling rivalry exist in your family or in a family with which you are familiar? How can individual family members work together to minimize ill effects of this typical conflict?

42. Compare and contrast Rass Island and/or Truitt, Virginia to where you live. In what ways are they similar? Different?

Quotations
1. "I love Rass Island, although for much of my life, I did not think I did."

2. "You were a good baby. You never gave us a minute's worry."

3. "But where was I? When everybody was working over Caroline, where was I?"

4. "Mercy, Wheeze, you stink like a crab shanty!"

5. "The Japanese have invaded America!"

6. "I feel sir, that under the circumstances, we should cancel Christmas."

7. "I hate the water." "I love the Lord."

8. "I see, if I want you I just call 'Call'."

9. "I had a bad dream. I dreamed you were dead."

10. "You never did think I was much to brag about, now did you?"

11. "Seventh? Seventh? Seventh don't have neither to do with hammering on Sunday. Seventh is the one on . . . adultery.

Jacob Have I Loved Extra Discussion Questions page 5

12. "Call I know those blasted commandments as well as you do and there is not one word in them about how to speak to tom cats. Now stop trying to play preacher and help me catch that damn cat and let's get him out of here."

13. "Old Captain Braxton had plenty, but he never let on. He let his wife and child scrimp by on next to nothing. Trudy found the money after they both died. And it scared her something silly to suddenly find all this cash, so she came running to my mother. My mother treated her like she was her own daughter. Poor Momma, she never gave up hoping I'd marry Trudy."

14. "It's all right, Trudy, it's me. I'll take care of you."

15. "Drown them? Just take them out and throw them in?"

16. "They sounded just like little babies."

17. "Oh, Jesus, you told the storm on Galilee, 'Peace, be still,' and it obeyed your word. Ohhhh, Lord, come down now and quiet this evil wind."

18. "T'aint fitting a heathen should read the Word of God."

19. "Oh my blessed, and here I was thinking how lucky we were. Is it clean gone?"

20. "Letting that heathen into our house. Into my bed. Oh, my blessed, into my very bed."

21. "Can't keep her eyes off that wicked man. I see it. Deed I do."

22. "Okay, Take it! Take it! Take everything I own."

23. "Don't call me Wheeze! I'm a person, not a disease symptom."

24. "Sara Louise, what's, the matter dear?"

25. "For goodness' sakes, Wheeze, it's only a game.

26. "We must convince him, Miss Susan. Sara Louise, tell her how you were saying to me just the other day that someone should understand that special circumstances demand special solutions-that Caroline ought to be sent to a really good school where she could continue her music. Isn't that right, Sara Louise?"

Jacob Have I Loved Extra Discussion Questions page 6

27. "As it is written, Jacob have I loved, but Esau have I hated."

28. "Crisfield! I'd rather be chopped for crab bait."

29. "The crabs now, they don't crave music, but oysters, there's nothing they favor more than a purty tune.

30. "Crabby as ever, I see, get it?"

31. "Let's just say she answered her Call."

32. "He thinks he's the cat's pajamas. Too good for the daughter of a man who don't even own his own boat."

33. "Youth is a mortal wound."

34. "You were never meant to be a woman on this island. A man perhaps, never a woman."

35. "You can do anything you want to. I've known that from the first day I met you-at the other end of my periscope."

36. "God in heaven what a stupid waste!"

37. "I chose to leave my own people and build a life for myself somewhere else."

38. "I was a bit of a romantic. I wanted to get away from what I thought of as a very conventional small town and try my wings."

39. "Will you really? As much as you miss Caroline?"

40. "God in heaven's been raising you for this valley from the day you were born."

41. "You should hold him. Hold him as much as you can or let his mother hold him."

LESSON SEVENTEEN

Objective
1. To complete discussions begun in Lessons Fifteen and Sixteen
2. To allow students time to complete extra activities of their choice
3. To give students the opportunity to share the stories of their birth

Activity #1
Since Lesson Fifteen and part of Lesson Sixteen were taken up with giving students time to formulate answers, you will need this class period to complete your class discussions.

Activity #2
Allow students to select an activity of their choice from the extra activities in the unit resource section. Also encourage students to create an activity of their own that corresponds to this unit.

Activity #3
Give students who would like to share Writing Assignment #3 the opportunity to read these orally. Encourage the use of personal baby props.

LESSON EIGHTEEN

Objective
To review all of the vocabulary work done in this unit

Activity
Choose one (or more) of the vocabulary review activities listed on the next page(s) and spend your class period as directed in the activity. Some of the materials for these review activities are located in the Vocabulary Resource section of this unit.

VOCABULARY REVIEW ACTIVITIES

1. Divide your class into two teams and have an old-fashioned spelling or definition bee.

2. Give each of your students (or students in groups of two, three or four) a *Jacob Have I Loved* Vocabulary Word Search Puzzle. The person (group) to find all of the vocabulary words in the puzzle first wins.

3. Give students a *Jacob Have I Loved* Vocabulary Word Search Puzzle without the word list. The person or group to find the most vocabulary words in the puzzle wins.

4. Use a *Jacob Have I Loved* Vocabulary Crossword Puzzle. Put the puzzle onto a transparency on the overhead projector (so everyone can see it), and do the puzzle together as a class.

5. Give students a *Jacob Have I Loved* Vocabulary Matching Worksheet to do.

6. Divide your class into two teams. Use the *Jacob Have I Loved* vocabulary words with their letters jumbled as a word list. Student 1 from Team A faces off against Student 1 from Team B. You write the first jumbled word on the board. The first student (1A or 1B) to unscramble the word wins the chance for his/her team to score points. If 1A wins the jumble, go to student 2A and give him/her a definition. He/she must give you the correct spelling of the vocabulary word which fits that definition. If he/she does, Team A scores a point, and you give student 3A a definition for which you expect a correctly spelled matching vocabulary word. Continue giving Team A definitions until some team member makes an incorrect response. An incorrect response sends the game back to the jumbled-word face off, this time with students 2A and 2B. Instead of repeating giving definitions to the first few students of each team, continue with the student after the one who gave the last incorrect response on the team. For example, if Team B wins the jumbled-word face-off, and student 5B gave the last incorrect answer for Team B, you would start this round of definition questions with student 6B, and so on. The team with the most points wins!

7. Have students write a story in which they correctly use as many vocabulary words as possible. Have students read their compositions orally. Post the most original compositions on your bulletinboard.

LESSON NINETEEN

Objective
To review the main ideas presented in *Jacob Have I Loved*

Activity #1
Choose one of the review games/activities included in the packet and spend your class period as outlined there. Some materials for these activities are located in the Extra Activities Packet section of this unit.

Activity #2
Remind students that the Unit Test will be in the next class meeting. Stress the review of the Study Guides and their class notes as a last minute, brush-up review for the unit test.

REVIEW GAMES/ACTIVITIES - *Jacob Have I Loved*

1. Ask the class to make up a unit test for *Jacob Have I Loved*. The test should have 4 sections: matching, true/false, short answer, and essay. Students may use 1/2 period to make the test and then swap papers and use the other 1/2 class period to take a test a classmate has devised. (open book) You may want to use the unit test included in this packet or take questions from the students' unit tests to formulate your own test.

2. Take 1/2 period for students to make up true and false questions (including the answers). Collect the papers and divide the class into two teams. Draw a big tic-tac-toe board on the chalk board. Make one team X and one team O. Ask questions to each side, giving each student one turn. If the question is answered correctly, that students' team's letter (X or O) is placed in the box. If the answer is incorrect, no mark is placed in the box. The object is to get three marks in a row like tic-tac-toe. You may want to keep track of the number of games won for each team.

3. Take 1/2 period for students to make up questions (true/false and short answer). Collect the questions. Divide the class into two teams. You'll alternate asking questions to individual members of teams A & B (like in a spelling bee). The question keeps going from A to B until it is correctly answered, then a new question is asked. A correct answer does not allow the team to get another question. Correct answers are +2 points; incorrect answers are -1 point.

4. Have students pair up and quiz each other from their study guides and class notes.

5. Give students a *Jacob Have I Loved* crossword puzzle to complete.

6. Divide your class into two teams. Use the *Jacob Have I Loved* crossword words with their letters jumbled as a word list. Student 1 from Team A faces off against Student 1 from Team B. You write the first jumbled word on the board. The first student (1A or 1B) to unscramble the word wins the chance for his/her team to score points. If 1A wins the jumble, go to student 2A and give him/her a clue. He/she must give you the correct word which matches that clue. If he/she does, Team A scores a point, and you give student 3A a clue for which you expect another correct response. Continue giving Team A clues until some team member makes an incorrect response. An incorrect response sends the game back to the jumbled-word face off, this time with students 2A and 2B. Instead of repeating giving clues to the first few students of each team, continue with the student after the one who gave the last incorrect response on the team. For example, if Team B wins the jumbled-word face-off, and student 5B gave the last incorrect answer for Team B, you would start this round of clue questions with student 6B, and so on.

UNIT TESTS

SHORT ANSWER UNIT TEST #1 - *Jacob Have I Loved*

I. Matching/Identify

___ Portia Sue   A. religion of the island
___ Rass   B. musically gifted Bradshaw twin
___ Sara Louise   C. island setting of novel
___ Truitt   D. streets of Rass
___ Caroline   E. nearest town by ferry
___ Methodism   F. Mr. Bradshaw's skipjack
___ Crisfield   G. islander who returns after 50 years
___ Juilliard   H. mountain-locked Virginia valley
___ Hiram Wallace   I. male blue crab
___ oyster-shell   J. New York music conservatory
___ tonging   K. method of crabbing
___ Jimmy   L. twin who chooses to become a midwife
___ progging   M. Caroline's husband
___ McCall Purnell   N. method of oystering

II. Short Answer

1. Describe the island from the speaker's point of view.

Jacob Have I Loved Short Answer Unit Test 1 Page 2

2. How does the story of Caroline and her birth make Wheeze feel?

3. On whom does Wheeze blame her unhappiness?

4. Why do the women of Rass hate the water?

5. What suggestion does Wheeze make to Mr. Rice at school and what is his reaction?

6. What story emerges from the past about Hiram Wallace?

7. Why does Wheeze fly into a wounded rage at Caroline and for what does she look for in the Bible?

8. How does Wheeze respond to the letter from LYRICS UNLIMITED?

Jacob Have I Loved Short Answer Unit Test 1 page 3

9. Why does Wheeze want to throw a jar of green beans at Grandma?

10. The Captain brings what news to the Bradshaws after Trudy dies, and how does it make Wheeze feel?

11. Grandma taunts Sara Louise with "As it is written, Jacob have I loved, but Esau have I hated." What does Wheeze do and explain what it means.

12. Working the water with her father, gives Wheeze an opportunity to think about the sooks. What is she thinking and who is she really thinking of?

13. Call's return visit brings some startling news for Wheeze. What was it?

14. Explain what the Captain meant by, "Youth is a mortal wound."

Jacob Have I Loved Short Answer Unit Test 1 page 4

15. While washing the windows with her mother, why does Wheeze become furious? What word of her mother's allows her to leave the island?

16. To what does Wheeze compare Truitt?

17. How does Sara Louise, the midwife, treat the twins she delivers?

Jacob Have I Loved Short Answer Unit Test 1 page 5

III. Essay

How and through which character does Katherine Paterson reveal the struggles of adolescence? Explain in detail citing examples from the novel to support your opinion.

IV. Vocabulary

Listen to the vocabulary words and spell them. After you have spelled all the words, go back and write down the definitions.

1.

2.

3.

4.

5.

6.

7.

8.

9.

10.

KEY: SHORT ANSWER UNIT TEST #1 - *Jacob Have I Loved*

I. Matching/Identify

- _F_ Portia Sue
- _C_ Rass
- _L_ Sara Louise
- _H_ Truitt
- _B_ Caroline
- _A_ Methodism
- _E_ Crisfield
- _J_ Juilliard
- _G_ Hiram Wallace
- _D_ oyster-shell
- _N_ tonging
- _I_ Jimmy
- _K_ progging
- _M_ McCall Purnell

A. religion of the island
B. musically gifted Bradshaw twin
C. island setting of novel
D. streets of Rass
E. nearest town by ferry
F. Mr. Bradshaw's skipjack
G. islander who returns after 50 years
H. mountain-locked Virginia valley
I. male blue crab
J. New York music conservatory
K. method of crabbing
L. twin who chooses to become a midwife
M. Caroline's husband
N. method of oystering

II. Short Answer

1. Describe the island from the speaker's point of view.
   It is a low lying island on the faded olive water of the Chesapeake with a church and cluster of white board houses being the first sight from the ferry. Mazes of docks, each with an islander's skipjack tied to it dot the harbor. Near the ferry house is Kellam's General Store, painted green and housing the post office. Behind it are the houses with their picket fences. The village only covers one-third of the island, the rest is salt marsh.

2. How does the story of Caroline and her birth make Wheeze feel?
   She feels cold all over, as though she was the newborn infant a second time, cast aside and forgotten.

3. On whom does Wheeze blame her unhappiness?
   She blames her unhappiness primarily on Caroline, then her grandmother, her mother, and even herself.

4. Why do the women of Rass hate the water?
   The island women see the water as the wild, untamed kingdom of their men and they try to resist its power over them.

5. What suggestion does Wheeze make to Mr. Rice at school and what is his reaction?
   She suggests they cancel the Christmas program due to all the suffering and dying because of the U. S.'s recent involvement in the war. He says thousands were suffering and dying when Christ was born and he continues the Christmas program practice.

6. What story emerges from the past about Hiram Wallace?
   The old people told the story that Captain Wallace and his son, Hiram, had let down their sails and were waiting out a storm in the Bay, using the sail for protection. Hiram feared lightening would strike the tall mast of his father's skipjack, so he rushed out from under his sail cover, took an axe, and chopped the mast to the level of the deck. They were sighted drifting mastless on the Bay after the storm, and were towed home. When everyone found out what he had done, he became the butt of all the watermen's jokes and left the island.

7. Why does Wheeze fly into a wounded rage at Caroline and for what does she look for in the Bible?
   She resents Caroline's remarks about how dirty her fingernails are after a day of crabbing. She searches for some shred of evidence that she will not be eternally damned for hating her sister.

8. How does Wheeze respond to the letter from LYRICS UNLIMITED?
   She is heartsick, rips it up, and flings it into the Bay.

9. Why does Wheeze want to throw a jar of green beans at Grandma?
   She is upset because her Grandmother notices her attraction to the old man and quotes scripture about it.

10. The Captain brings what news to the Bradshaws after Trudy dies, and how does it make Wheeze feel?
    He joyfully brought the news that he had investigated how much a good music boarding school in Baltimore would cost for Caroline, and Trudy's legacy would be enough to cover it. Wheeze feels betrayed and cheated out of something she deserved.

11. Grandma taunts Sara Louise with a verse from the Bible, " As it is written, Jacob have I loved, but Esau have I hated" until Wheeze does what? What does it mean?
    Wheeze goes to the Bible and locates the verse to determine who says it. From Romans, the ninth chapter and the thirteenth verse she finds that it is God who says it. She feels that God, himself hates her too. The Biblical tale is one in which Esau, the elder twin is cheated out of his birthright by his conniving brother Jacob, and their mother Rebecca. Wheeze has hated this story from childhood.

12. Working the water with her father, gives Wheeze an opportunity to think about the sooks. Of what is she thinking and of whom is she really thinking?

    She thinks that the ordinary, ungifted ones just get soft and die. She is thinking of her ungifted self.

13. Call's return visit brings some startling news for Wheeze. What was it?

    He has proposed marriage to her twin sister, Caroline.

14. Explain what the Captain meant by, "Youth is a mortal wound."

    The Captain meant that he was content in his old age and it was "good" to be old.

15. While washing the windows with her mother, why does Wheeze become furious? What word of her mother's allows her to leave the island?

    Wheeze discovers that her mother used to write poetry and wanted to go to Paris, but instead came to Rass to teach. It is an insult to Wheeze to think her mother chose the life she leads on the island over something far more stimulating. Her mother tells her if she leaves the island her father and she will miss her. Wheeze asks if they will miss her as much as they miss Caroline. Her mother responds with, "More."

16. To what does Wheeze compare Truitt?

    She compares it to an island. The Appalachian wilderness is like an island's water, and their jeeps are like the boats on Rass. Most residents seldom leave its boundaries.

17. How does Sara Louise, the midwife, treat the twins she delivers?

    She wants to give equal attention to both babies, but the smaller one requires more. She is stricken with the realization that she has forgotten the healthier one, the boy, who is resting alone in the basket. She admonishes the family to hold him, the first born, as well as the smaller, frailer girl.

III. Essay

Grade the essays on your own criteria.

IV. Vocabulary

Choose ten of the vocabulary words to read orally for the vocabulary section of this unit test.

SHORT ANSWER UNIT TEST 2 *Jacob Have I Loved*

I. Matching/Identify

___ Portia Sue   A. island setting of novel
___ Rass   B. method of oystering
___ Sara Louise   C. Caroline's husband
___ Truitt   D. streets of Rass
___ Caroline   E. male blue crab
___ Methodism   F. religion of the island
___ Crisfield   G. musically gifted Bradshaw twin
___ Juilliard   H. mountain-locked Virginia valley
___ Hiram Wallace   I. nearest town by ferry
___ oyster-shell   J. New York music conservatory
___ tonging   K. method of crabbing
___ Jimmy   L. twin who chooses to become a midwife
___ progging   M. Mr. Bradshaw's skipjack
___ McCall Purnell   N. islander who returns after 50 years

II. Short Answer

1. Where is Rass Island located?

2. What do the watermen's boats look like and for whom are they named?

3. How does the story of Caroline's and her birth make Wheeze feel?

4. For what does Wheeze pray?

Jacob Have I Loved Short Answer Unit Test 2 Page 2

5. What event did Wheeze hear about on the radio Sunday, December 7, 1941?

6. What story emerges from the past about Hiram Wallace?

7. How does Wheeze plan to leave the island?

8. What does the Captain say that finally gets Wheeze to laugh?

9. What unknown fact about Trudy does the Captain share with Call and Wheeze?

10. How do the Bradshaws prepare for the storm?

11. What action does Wheeze take to comfort the Captain?

12. Why does Wheeze want to throw a jar of green beans at Grandma?

Jacob Have I Loved Short Answer Unit Test 2 Page 3

13. Why does Wheeze become jealous of Call?

14. The Captain brings what news that causes Wheeze to feel betrayed?

15. Call's return for a visit brings some startling news for Wheeze. What was it?

16. What information about herself does Wheeze share with the Captain?

17. What one word of her mother's allows Wheeze to finally leave the island? Explain.

18. Why does Wheeze choose a town named Truitt, Virginia to begin her career?

Jacob Have I Loved Short Answer Unit Test 2 Page 4

III. Quotations: Identify the speaker and explain the significance of these quotes:

1. "Mercy, Wheeze, you stink like a crab shanty!"

2. "Seventh? Seventh? Seventh don't have neither to do with hammering on Sunday. Seventh is the one on .... adultery."

3. "Oh, Jesus, you told the storm on Galilee, 'Peace, be still', and it obeyed your word. Ohhhh, Lord, come down now and quiet this evil wind."

4. "Oh my blessed, and here I was thinking how lucky we were. Is it clean gone?"

5. "Can't keep her eyes off that wicked man. I see it. Deed I do."

6. "Okay, Take it! Take it! Take everything I own."

7. "I was a bit of a romantic. I wanted to get away from what I thought of as a very conventional small town and try my wings.

8. "As it is written, Jacob have I loved, but Esau have I hated."

9. "Youth is a mortal wound."

10. "God in heaven what a stupid waste!"

11. "You were never meant to be a woman on this island. A man perhaps, never a woman."

Jacob Have I Loved Short Answer Unit Test 2 page 5

IV. Vocabulary

Listen to the vocabulary words and spell them. After you have spelled all the words, go back and write down the definitions.

1.

2.

3.

4.

5.

6.

7.

8.

9.

10.

KEY: SHORT ANSWER UNIT TEST 2 *Jacob Have I Loved*

I. Matching

_M_	Portia Sue	A. island setting of novel
_A_	Rass	B. method of oystering
_L_	Sara Louise	C. Caroline's husband
_H_	Truitt	D. streets of Rass
_G_	Caroline	E. male blue crab
_F_	Methodism	F. religion of the island
_I_	Crisfield	G. musically gifted Bradshaw twin
_J_	Juilliard	H. mountain-locked Virginia valley
_N_	Hiram Wallace	I. nearest town by ferry
_D_	oyster-shell	J. New York music conservatory
_B_	tonging	K. method of crabbing
_E_	Jimmy	L. twin who chooses to become a midwife
_K_	progging	M. Mr. Bradshaw's skipjack
_C_	McCall Purnell	N. islander who returns after 50 years

II. Short Answer

1. Where is Rass Island located?
    Rass is located in the Chesapeake Bay of Maryland near Crisfireld.

2. What do the watermen's boats look like and for whom are they named?
    Each has a small cabin toward the bow, washboards wide enough for a man to stand on running from the point of the bow to the stern. Near the winch that pulls the line of pots up from the Bay bottom is a large washtub into which all the harvest is deposited and then sorted. Each boat bears a woman's name, usually the waterman's mother or grandmother, depending on how long the boat has been in the family.

3. How does the story of Caroline's and her birth make Wheeze feel?
    She feels cold all over, like she was the newborn infant a second time, cast aside and forgotten

4. For what does Wheeze pray?
    Wheeze prays to turn into a boy so she can work the water with her father.

5. What event did Wheeze hear about on the radio Sunday, December 7, 1941?
    The bombing of Pearl Harbor by the Japanese.

6. What story emerges from the past about Hiram Wallace?
   The old people told the story that Captain Wallace and his son, Hiram, had let down their sails and were waiting out a storm in the bay, using the sail for protection. Hiram feared lightening would strike the tall mast of his father's skipjack, so he rushed out from under his sail cover, took an axe, and chopped the mast to the level of the deck. They were sighted drifting mastless on the bay after the storm, and were towed home. When everyone found out what he had done, he became the butt of all the watermen's jokes and left the island.

7. How does Wheeze plan to leave the island?
   She plans to double her crab catch and keep half the money for herself, as well as make money on her poetry.

8. What does the Captain say that finally gets Wheeze to laugh?
   He tells Call there isn't any commandment about how to speak to tom cats.

9. What unknown fact about Trudy does the Captain share with Call and Wheeze?
   Trudy's father left her a substantial sum of cash.

10. How do the Bradshaws prepare for the storm?
    They board up the windows, carry canned goods upstairs, and the father sank his boat.

11. What action does Wheeze take to comfort the Captain?
    She embraces him.

12. Why does Wheeze want to throw a jar of green beans at Grandma?
    She is upset because Grandma notices her attraction to Hiram and quotes scripture.

13. Why does Wheeze become jealous of Call?
    He has now been able to quit school and work with her father.

14. The Captain brings what news that causes Wheeze to feel betrayed?
    He is able to send Caroline to music school with Trudy's legacy.

15. Grandma taunts Sara Louise with a verse from the Bible, " As it is written, Jacob have I loved, Esau have I hated" until Wheeze does what? What does it mean?
    It is based on the Biblical scripture about Esau, the elder son of Isaac, who is cheated out of his birthright by his younger twin brother, Jacob and their mother Rebecca. Grandma sees this situation similar to it and quotes it to Wheeze.

16. Call's return for a visit brings some startling news for Wheeze. What was it?
    He has proposed to her twin sister, Caroline.

17. Why does the Captain say, "Youth is a mortal wound."
    He is content to be old and has regrets about his youth.

18. What information about herself does Wheeze share with the Captain?
    She would like to be a doctor.

19. What one word of her mother's allows Wheeze to finally leave the island? Explain.
    Wheeze asks her mother if they'll miss her as much as they miss Caroline and her mother says, "more."

20. Why does Wheeze choose a town named Truitt, Virginia to begin her career?
    It is in the mountains and that is her father's name.

III. Quotations Answers will depend on your class discussions of these quotations.

IV. Vocabulary
    Choose ten of the vocabulary words to read orally for the vocabulary section of the test.

ADVANCED SHORT ANSWER UNIT TEST - *Jacob Have I Loved*

I. Matching

___ Portia Sue   A. island setting of novel
___ Rass   B. method of oystering
___ Sara Louise   C. Caroline's husband
___ Truitt   D. streets of Rass
___ Caroline   E. male blue crab
___ Methodism   F. religion of the island
___ Crisfield   G. musically gifted Bradshaw twin
___ Juilliard   H. mountain-locked Virginia valley
___ Hiram Wallace   I. nearest town by ferry
___ oyster-shell   J. New York music conservatory
___ tonging   K. method of crabbing
___ Jimmy   L. twin who chooses to become a midwife
___ progging   M. Mr. Bradshaw's skipjack
___ McCall Purnell   N. islander who returns after 50 years

II. Short Answer

1. Explain the significance of the title "*Jacob Have I Loved.*"

Jacob Have I Loved Advanced Short Answer Unit Test Page 2

2. Who is responsible for Wheeze finally leaving the island? Defend your answer.

3. When Wheeze is actually presented with an offer to go to boarding school in Crisfield, she furiously refuses. Why did she react in that manner when earlier that was her primary goal?

4. Essie's first-born twin, the healthy baby, was a boy. Do you think this was intentional on the author's part? Why or why not?

5. What universal themes are present in *Jacob Have I Loved*?

6. How does Wheeze seem to come full circle by the end of the novel concerning her birth, abilities, and her sister? Cite evidence to support you opinions.

Jacob Have I Loved Advanced Short Answer Unit Test Page 3

III. Quotations: Explain the importance and meaning of the following quotations.

1. "Okay, Take it! Take it! Take everything I own."

2. "We must convince him, Miss Susan. Sara Louise, tell her how you were saying to me just the other day that someone should understand that special circumstances demand special solutions-that Caroline ought to be sent to a really good school where she could continue her music. Isn't that right, Sara Louise?"

3. "As it is written, Jacob have I loved, but Esau have I hated."

4. "Youth is a mortal wound."

5. "You were never meant to be a woman on this island. A man perhaps, never a woman."

6. "God in heaven what a stupid waste!"

7. "God in heaven's been raising you for this valley from the day you were born."

Jacob Have I Loved Advanced Short Answer Unit Test Page 4

IV. Vocabulary

Listen to the vocabulary words and write them down. After you have written down all the words, write a paragraph in which you use all the words. The paragraph must in some way relate to *Jacob Have I Loved*.

MULTIPLE CHOICE-MATCHING TEST #1 *Jacob Have I Loved*

I. Matching

1 Portia Sue   A. religion of the island

2 Rass   B. musically gifted Bradshaw twin

3 Sara Louise   C. island setting of novel

4 Truitt   D. streets of Rass

5 Caroline   E. nearest town by ferry

6 Methodism   F. Mr. Bradshaw's skipjack

7 Crisfield   G. islander who returns after 50 years

8 Juilliard   H. mountain-locked Virginia valley

9 Hiram Wallace   I. male blue crab

10 oyster-shell   J. New York music conservatory

11 tonging   K. method of crabbing

12 Jimmy   L. twin who chooses to become a midwife

13 progging   M. Caroline's husband

14 McCall Purnell   N. method of oystering

II. Multiple Choice

1. Rass Island is described as
    a. one-third of the land is village
    b. a salt marsh
    c. having lots of docks and boats
    d. all of the above

2. The story of their birth makes Wheeze feel
    a. cold and neglected
    b. warm and cozy
    c. nostalgic
    d. anxious

Jacob Have I Loved Multiple Choice Unit Test 1 page 2

3. Wheeze blames her unhappiness on herself and
    a. her mother
    b. her Grandma
    c. Caroline
    d. all of the above

4. Wheeze suggests to Mr. Rice at school that they
    a. cancel Christmas
    b. go Christmas carolling
    c. join the Navy
    d. volunteer for the Salvation Army

5. Mr. Rice responds to her suggestion by
    a. agreeing with her
    b. ignoring her
    c. dismissing her suggestion and continuing practice
    d. deciding to take a class vote

6. The women of Rass hate the water because
    a. they can't see the bottom
    b. of the sharks
    c. they can't swim
    d. they resent its power over their lives

7. What story emerges from the past about Hiram Wallace?
    a. He became a doctor and discovered a cure for malaria.
    b. He cut down his daddy's mast during a storm.
    c. He fell off the ferry and had amnesia.
    d. He ran off on his wedding day.

8. Wheeze flies into a wounded rage at Caroline because
    a. Caroline won't share dessert.
    b. Caroline remarks how dirty her fingernails are.
    c. Caroline borrows her best dress without asking.
    d. Caroline steals her boyfriend.

Jacob Have I Loved Multiple Choice Unit Test 1 page 3

9. Wheeze searches in the Bible for
    a. Proverbs
    b. evidence that she won't be damned for hating her sister
    c. the Lord's Prayer
    d. a Psalm to read to Grandma

10. Wheeze responds to the letter from LYRICS UNLIMITED by
    a. mailing them more poems
    b. writing back immediately
    c. sending them money
    d. tearing the letter into bits

11. Wheeze wants to throw a jar of green beans at Grandma because
    a. Grandma notices her attraction to the Captain and quotes scripture about it
    b. Wheeze wants her bedroom
    c. Wheeze hates the dinner Grandma wants

12. What news does the Captain bring that causes Wheeze to feel betrayed?
    a. He will donate Trudy's legacy to the SPCA in Baltimore.
    b. He wants to adopt Call.
    c. He wants to send Caroline to music school in Baltimore.
    d. Trudy left her money to the church.

13. What does the scripture Grandma quotes to Wheeze mean to Wheeze?
    a. Jacob loves her
    b. God hates Jacob
    c. Esau hates Jacob
    d. God hates her
    e. both a and c

14. While sorting crabs, Wheeze feels great empathy for the sooks. Whom is she thinking of?
    a. herself
    b. Grandma
    c. her mother
    d. Trudy

Jacob Have I Loved Multiple Choice Unit Test 1 page 4

15. Call's return for a visit brings some startling news for Wheeze. What was it?
    a. He has proposed to Caroline.
    b. He was wounded in the South Pacific.
    c. He has re-enlisted for another four years in the Navy.
    d. He asks her to marry him.

16. Why does the Captain say, "Youth is a mortal wound?"
    a. He hates that he is old now.
    b. He's content to be old, rather than struggling with youth.
    c. He shot someone by mistake when he was young.
    d. He wants to be young again.

17. Wheeze becomes furious while washing windows with her mother because
    a. she shares that she was married before
    b. she makes her do the neighbor's windows
    c. she chose Rass over Paris
    d. Grandma is bossing them around and her mother just takes it

18. What one word of her mother's allows her to finally leave the island?
    a. more
    b. yes
    c. less
    d. love

19. She compares this mountain-locked valley to
    a. a piece of heaven
    b. an island
    c. a desert
    d. a peninsula

20. How does Wheeze treat the twin babies she delivers?
    a. She gives more attention to the first-born boy.
    b. She gives more attention to the smaller, second-born baby girl.
    c. She treats them both equally.
    d. She is impatient and needs to get home to her own baby.

Jacob Have I Loved Multiple Choice Unit Test 1 page 5

III. Quotations: Identify the speaker:

A= Sara Louise B= Caroline C= Call D= Hiram Wallace

E= Grandma F= Truitt G= Susan

1. "Mercy, Wheeze, you stink like a crab shanty!"

2. "Seventh? Seventh? Seventh don't have neither to do with hammering on Sunday. Seventh is the one on .... adultery."

3. "Oh, Jesus, you told the storm on Galilee, 'Peace, be still', and it obeyed your word. Ohhhh, Lord, come down now and quiet this evil wind."

4. "Oh my blessed, And here I was thinking how lucky we were. Is it clean gone?"

5. "Can't keep her eyes off that wicked man. I see it. Deed I do."

6. "Okay, Take it! Take it! Take everything I own."

7. "I chose to leave my own people and build a life for myself somewhere else."

8. "As it is written, Jacob have I loved, but Esau have I hated."

9. "Youth is a mortal wound."

10. "God in heaven what a stupid waste!"

11. "You were never meant to be a woman on this island. A man perhaps, never a woman."

12. "I was a bit of a romantic. I wanted to get away from what I thought of as a very conventional small town and try my wings."

Jacob Have I Loved Multiple Choice Unit Test 1 page 6

IV. Vocabulary (Matching)

1. contentious   A. erratic; unpredictable
2. diminished   B. scheming
3. benevolently   C. quirks; abnormalities
4. futile   D. quarrelsome
5. aberrations   E. hopeless
6. capricious   F. irritable or ill tempered; peevish
7. conniving   G. removed
8. deprivation   H. loss
9. discomposure   I. shell fragments from an explosion
10. fervent   J. abandonment; denial
11. petulant   K. kindly
12. pretentious   L. threatening
13. scrutiny   M. small stream
14. rankle   N. irritate or cause resentment
15. renunciation   O. unchanging; strict
16. shrapnel   P. puffed up; self-important
17. extricated   Q. awkwardness
18. rivulet   R. showing great emotion or zeal
19. unrelenting   S. made smaller; lessened
20. ominous   T. examination; close attention

MULTIPLE CHOICE-MATCHING UNIT TEST #2 - *Jacob Have I Loved*

I. Matching

1. Jimmy
2. Hiram Wallace
3. Truitt
4. McCall Purnell
5. Caroline
6. Portia Sue
7. Juilliard
8. tonging
9. Crisfield
10. Methodism
11. oyster-shell
12. Sara Louise
13. Rass
14. progging

A. religion of the island
B. musically gifted Bradshaw twin
C. island setting of novel
D. streets of Rass
E. nearest town by ferry
F. Mr. Bradshaw's skipjack
G. islander who returns after 50 years
H. mountain-locked Virginia valley
I. male blue crab
J. New York music conservatory
K. method of crabbing
L. twin who chooses to become a midwife
M. Caroline's husband
N. method of oystering

II. Multiple Choice

1. Rass Island located in
    a. Hawaii
    b. Chesapeake Bay
    c. Cape Cod
    d. Bay of Biscay

2. The watermen's boats
    a. have a small cabin
    b. have wide washboards
    c. have barrels and buckets lying around
    d. all of the above

Jacob Have I Loved Short Answer Unit Test 2 Page 2

3. The waterman's boats are named for
    a. their girlfriends
    b. their fathers
    c. their mothers or wives
    d. themselves

4. The story of their birth makes Wheeze feel
    a. pleased
    b. nostalgic
    c. warm and cozy
    d. cold and neglected

5. Wheeze prays
    a. to become a boy
    b. to be prettier
    c. to be able to sing like Caroline
    d. to lose weight

6. What event did Wheeze hear about on the radio Sunday, December 7, 1941?
    a. F.D.R.'s death
    b. D-day
    c. Pearl Harbor
    d. V-E Day

7. What story emerges from the past about Hiram Wallace?
    a. He became a doctor and discovered a cure for malaria.
    b. He ran off on his wedding day.
    c. He fell off the ferry and had amnesia for forty years.
    d. He cut down the mast of his daddy's boat during a storm.

8. Wheeze plans to leave the island by
    a. making enough money to go to school in Crisfield
    b. taking the ferry to Salisbury
    c. running away
    d. swimming to a sandbar and waiting for a boat

Jacob Have I Loved Short Answer Unit Test 2 Page 3

9. What does the Captain say that finally gets Wheeze to laugh?
    a. He tells Call there's nothing in the Bible about how to talk to tom cats.
    b. He says "Dagnabit".
    c. He tells a joke about F.D.R. thinking he's God.
    d. He reminds them of their first meeting.

10. The Captain shares with Call and Wheeze that Trudy
    a. was once his wife
    b. inherited a lot of money
    c. is Catholic
    d. is half-deaf

11. The Bradshaws prepare for the storm by
    a. boarding up the windows
    b. bringing up the canned goods
    c. both a and b

12. To comfort the Captain, Wheeze
    a. bails out his boat
    b. embraces him
    c. gives him a present
    d. smiles and pats him on the back

13. Wheeze wants to throw a jar of green beans at Grandma because
    a. Wheeze wants her bedroom back
    b. Grandma won't take her nap
    c. Grandma notices her attraction to the Captain and quotes scripture about it
    d. Caroline and she are laughing at her

14. Wheeze becomes jealous of Call because
    a. he gets to go to Crisfield to school
    b. he is working the water with her father
    c. he joins the Navy
    d. he gets an apartment

Jacob Have I Loved Short Answer Unit Test 2 Page 4

15. What news does the Captain bring that causes Wheeze to feel betrayed?
    a. He's going to adopt Call.
    b. Trudy left her money to the church.
    c. He'd like to send Caroline to music school in Baltimore.
    d. He is moving back to the mainland.

16. Call's returns for a visit with the startling news that
    a. he wants to marry Wheeze
    b. he has re-enlisted in the Navy
    c. he has lost a leg in the war
    d. he has proposed to Caroline

17. What goal about herself does Wheeze share with the Captain?
    a. She wants to marry Call.
    b. She wants to become a doctor.
    c. She wants to move to the mountains.
    d. She wants to go to music school like Caroline.

18. What one word of her mother's allows Wheeze to finally leave the island ?
    a. okay
    b. fine
    c. more
    d. love

19. After leaving the University of Maryland Wheeze goes to
    a. Salisbury State College
    b. Virginia Tech
    c. University of Kentucky
    d. Pennsylvania State University

20. Why does Wheeze choose a town named Truitt, Virginia to begin her career?
    a. It is far from Rass.
    b. It bears her father's name.
    c. It's in the mountains.
    d. Both b and c

Jacob Have I Loved Short Answer Unit Test 2 Page 5

III. Quotations: Identify the speaker:

A= Susan   B= Caroline   C= Grandma   D= Truitt

E= Call   F= Hiram Wallace   G= Sara Louise

1. "Mercy, Wheeze, you stink like a crab shanty!"

2. "Seventh? Seventh? Seventh don't have neither to do with hammering on Sunday. Seventh is the one on .... adultery."

3. "Oh, Jesus, you told the storm on Galilee, 'Peace, be still', and it obeyed your word. Ohhhh, Lord, come down now and quiet this evil wind."

4. "Oh my blessed, And here I was thinking how lucky we were. Is it clean gone?"

5. "Can't keep her eyes off that wicked man. I see it. Deed I do."

6. "Okay, Take it! Take it! Take everything I own."

7. "I chose to leave my own people and build a life for myself somewhere else."

8. "As it is written, Jacob have I loved, but Esau have I hated."

9. "Youth is a mortal wound."

10. "God in heaven what a stupid waste!"

11. "You were never meant to be a woman on this island. A man perhaps, never a woman."

12. "I was a bit of a romantic. I wanted to get away from what I thought of as a very conventional small town and try my wings."

Jacob Have I Loved Multiple Choice Unit Test 2 page 6

IV. Vocabulary (Matching)

1. futile	A. loss
2. diminished	B. scheming
3. capricious	C. quirks; abnormalities
4. contentious	D. removed
5. fervent	E. erratic; unpredictable
6. petulant	F. irritable or ill tempered; peevish
7. conniving	G. quarrelsome
8. deprivation	H. hopeless
9. benevolently	I. shell fragments from an explosion
10. aberrations	J. awkwardness
11. discomposure	K. kindly
12. shrapnel	L. threatening
13. rivulet	M. unchanging; strict
14. rankle	N. examination; close attention
15. renunciation	O. small stream
16. scrutiny	P. puffed up; self-important
17. ominous	Q. abandonment; denial
18. pretentious	R. showing great emotion or zeal
19. unrelenting	S. made smaller; lessened
20. extricated	T. irritate or cause resentment

ANSWER SHEET: MULTIPLE CHOICE UNIT TESTS - *Jacob Have I Loved*

I. Matching

1. ___
2. ___
3. ___
4. ___
5. ___
6. ___
7. ___
8. ___
9. ___
10. ___
11. ___
12. ___
13. ___
14. ___

II. Multiple Choice

1. (A) (B) (C) (D)
2. (A) (B) (C) (D)
3. (A) (B) (C) ( )
4. (A) (B) (C) (D)
5. (A) (B) (C) (D)
6. (A) (B) (C) (D)
7. (A) (B) (C) (D)
8. (A) (B) (C) (D)
9. (A) (B) (C) (D)
10. (A) (B) (C) (D)
11. (A) (B) (C) (D)
12. (A) (B) (C) (D)
13. (A) (B) (C) (D)
14. (A) (B) (C) (D)
15. (A) (B) (C) (D)
16. (A) (B) (C) (D)
17. (A) (B) (C) (D)
18. (A) (B) (C) (D)
19. (A) (B) (C) (D)
20. (A) (B) (C) (D)

III. Quotes

1. (A) (B) (C) (D) (E) (F) (G)
2. (A) (B) (C) (D) (E) (F) (G)
3. (A) (B) (C) (D) (E) (F) (G)
4. (A) (B) (C) (D) (E) (F) (G)
5. (A) (B) (C) (D) (E) (F) (G)
6. (A) (B) (C) (D) (E) (F) (G)
7. (A) (B) (C) (D) (E) (F) (G)
8. (A) (B) (C) (D) (E) (F) (G)
9. (A) (B) (C) (D) (E) (F) (G)
10. (A) (B) (C) (D) (E) (F) (G)
11. (A) (B) (C) (D) (E) (F) (G)
12. (A) (B) (C) (D) (E) (F) (G)

IV. Vocabulary

1. ___
2. ___
3. ___
4. ___
5. ___
6. ___
7. ___
8. ___
9. ___
10. ___
11. ___
12. ___
13. ___
14. ___
15. ___
16. ___
17. ___
18. ___
19. ___
20. ___

ANSWER SHEET KEY- *Jacob Have I Loved*
Multiple Choice Unit Test 1

I. Matching
1. F
2. C
3. L
4. H
5. B
6. A
7. E
8. J
9. G
10. D
11. N
12. I
13. K
14. M

II. Multiple Choice

1. (A) (B) (C) ( )
2. ( ) (B) (C) (D)
3. (A) (B) (C) (D)
4. ( ) (B) (C) (D)
5. (A) (B) ( ) (D)
6. (A) (B) (C) ( )
7. (A) ( ) (C) (D)
8. (A) ( ) (C) (D)
9. (A) ( ) (C) (D)
10 (A) (B) (C) ( )
11. ( ) (B) (C) (D)
12. (A) (B) ( ) (D)
13. (A) (B) (C) ( )
14. (A) (B) (C) ( )
15. ( ) (B) (C) (D)
16. (A) ( ) (C) (D)
17. (A) (B) ( ) (D)
18. ( ) (B) (C) (D)
19. (A) ( ) (C) (D)
20. (A) ( ) (C) (D)

III. Quotes
1. (A) ( ) (C) (D) (E) (F) (G)
2. (A) (B) ( ) (D) (E) (F) (G)
3. (A) (B) (C) (D) ( ) (F) (G)
4. (A) (B) (C) (D) (E) ( ) (G)
5. (A) (B) (C) (D) ( ) (F) (G)
6. ( ) (B) (C) (D) (E) (F) (G)
7. (A) (B) (C) (D) (E) (F) ( )
8. (A) (B) (C) (D) ( ) (F) (G)
9. (A) (B) (C) ( ) (E) (F) (G)
10. ( ) (B) (C) (D) (E) (F) (G)
11. (A) (B) (C) ( ) (E) (F) (G)
12. (A) (B) (C) (D) (E) (F) ( )

IV. Vocabulary
1. D
2. S
3. K
4. E
5. C
6. A
7. B
8. H
9. Q
10. R
11. D
12. P
13. T
14. N
15. J
16. I
17. G
18. M
19. O
20. L

ANSWER SHEET KEY - *Jacob Have I Loved*
Multiple Choice Unit Test 2

I. Matching
1. I
2. G
3. H
4. M
5. B
6. F
7. J
8. N
9. E
10. A
11. D
12. L
13. C
14. K

II. Multiple Choice

1. (A) ( ) (C) (D)
2. (A) (B) (C) ( )
3. (A) (B) ( ) (D)
4. (A) (B) (C) ( )
5. ( ) (B) (C) (D)
6. (A) (B) ( ) (D)
7. (A) (B) (C) ( )
8. ( ) (B) (C) (D)
9. ( ) (B) (C) (D)
10. (A) ( ) (C) (D)
11. (A) (B) ( ) (D)
12. (A) ( ) (C) (D)
13. (A) (B) ( ) (D)
14. (A) ( ) (C) (D)
15. (A) (B) ( ) (D)
16. (A) (B) (C) ( )
17. (A) ( ) (C) (D)
18. (A) (B) ( ) (D)
19. (A) (B) ( ) (D)
20. (A) (B) (C) ( )

III. Quotes
1. (A) ( ) (C) (D) (E) (F) (G)
2. (A) (B) (C) (D) ( ) (F) (G)
3. (A) (B) ( ) (D) (E) (F) (G)
4. (A) (B) (C) ( ) (E) (F) (G)
5. (A) (B) ( ) (D) (E) (F) (G)
6. (A) (B) (C) (D) (E) (F) ( )
7. ( ) (B) (C) (D) (E) (F) (G)
8. (A) (B) ( ) (D) (E) (F) (G)
9. (A) (B) (C) (D) (E) ( ) (G)
10. (A) (B) (C) (D) (E) (F) ( )
11. (A) (B) (C) (D) (E) ( ) (G)
12. ( ) (B) (C) (D) (E) (F) (G)

IV. Vocabulary
1. H
2. S
3. E
4. G
5. R
6. F
7. B
8. A
9. K
10. C
11. J
12. I
13. O
14. T
15. Q
16. N
17. L
18. P
19. M
20. D

UNIT RESOURCE MATERIALS

BULLETIN BOARD IDEAS - *Jacob Have I Loved*

1. Save a space for students' best writing. Make a nice border. Maybe something from the novel like crab shapes, or sea shells. Cut out letters YOU'RE THE CAT'S PAJAMAS! (Grandma's statement about Hiram) or something else to designate quality work. Use some visual (a cat wearing pj's?) to show the meaning of the space. Staple up the best writing samples (or quizzes or whatever you have graded) on colorful paper.

2. Bring in (or have students bring in) pictures of Bay or seashore life.. Make a collage if you have enough different pictures (or post individual pictures on colorful paper if you only have a few pictures). This could also be a fun introductory activity if students participate. You could have the border and title done for the bulletinboard and invite students to staple up their own pictures wherever they want them. It will only take a few minutes of class time, but the students will enjoy it and you can get your bulletinboard done in a hurry.

3. Draw one of the word search puzzles onto the bulletinboard. (Be sure to enlarge it.) Write the key words to one side. Invite students to take their pens or markers and find the words before and/or after class (or perhaps this could be an activity for students who finish their work early).

4. Have artistic students create a mural depicting Rass Island and/or Truitt, Virginia. Placing them side by side students can compare these settings. Less artistic, but interested students, could do the research from the novel and elsewhere to give to the artists for authenticity.

5. Research and display seafood recipes and pictures focusing on: crab, oyster, and terrapin recipes. Students could actually make these and share with class.

6. Illustrate Caroline and Wheeze and other sets of twins by either photos, silhouettes, portraits, or whatever your choice. Include information gained from interviewing sets of twins.

7. Post lyrics of the song Caroline sang, "I Wonder As I Wander" with its musical score. Have students illustrate the meaning of the lyrics.

8. Post and illustrate Wheeze's poetry and original poetry students have written, or recreate a row of front yards from Rass with the tombstone markers and elegies written on them. Students could write their own epitaphs for class members placing on tombstone markers.

9. Post and illustrate Wheeze's jokes and any others students want to display. You could have the questions written on the bulletinboard and then have the answers hidden under a flap or in an envelope that students could manipulate. Try a comedian class period, where any willing and able students try their skill at appropriate joke telling.

EXTRA ACTIVITIES

One of the difficulties in teaching a novel is that all students don't read at the same speed. One student who likes to read may take the book home and finish it in a day or two. Sometimes a few students finish the in-class assignments early. The problem, then, is finding suitable extra activities for students.

One thing that helps is to keep a little library in the classroom. For this unit on *Jacob Have I Loved*, you might check out from the school library other books by Katherine Paterson. A biography of the author would be interesting for some students. You may include other related books and articles about: twins, watermen, the dying tradition of following the water, the elderly, World War II, crabs and crabbing (especially *Beautiful Swimmers: Watermen, Crabs and the Chesapeake Bay* and *Follow the Water*) oysters and oystering, Chesapeake Bay, hurricanes, home schooling, ferries, music schools, espionage and codes or code books, etc.

Other things you may keep on hand are puzzles. We have made some relating directly to *Jacob Have I Loved* for you. Feel free to duplicate them for your students.

Some students may like to draw. You might devise a contest or allow some extra-credit grade for students who draw characters or scenes from *Jacob Have I Loved*. Note, too, that if the students do not want to keep their drawings you may pick up some extra bulletin board materials this way. If you have a contest and you supply the prize or, you could possibly make the drawing itself a non-refundable entry fee.

The pages which follow contain games, puzzles and worksheets. The keys, when appropriate, immediately follow the puzzle or worksheet. There are two main groups of activities: one group for the unit; that is, generally relating to the *Jacob Have I Loved* text, and another group of activities related strictly to the *Jacob Have I Loved* vocabulary.

Directions for the games, puzzles and worksheets are self-explanatory. The object here is to provide you with extra materials you may use in any way you choose.

MORE ACTIVITIES - *Jacob Have I Loved*

1. Pick a chapter or scene with a great deal of dialogue and have the students act it out on a stage. (Perhaps you could assign various scenes to different groups of students so more than one scene could be acted and more students could participate.)

2. Show the Wonder Works film version of *Jacob Have I Loved* to the class after you have completed reading the novel. Have students evaluate the movie and compare/contrast it with the book. If the students have tried writing a chapter into a scene in a play, you may wish to discuss how the problems they encountered in changing the form were handled in the movie.

3. Have students design a book cover (front and back and inside flaps) for *Jacob Have I Loved.*

4. Students could design wedding announcements for one or both weddings (Hiram and Trudy's; Call and Caroline's) in the novel.

5. Debate the effects of advertising on adolescent girls and boys. (Wheeze referred many times to her images not measuring up, *'She's lovely, she's engaged, she uses Pond's '*) Is there a bigger impact on one gender over the other?

6. Use some of the related topics (noted earlier for an in-class library) as topics for research, reports or written papers, or as topics for guest speakers.

7. Have students plan and teach a lesson on a chapter or section of the book. Give them guidelines and a timeframe.

8. Invite a professional manicurist to demonstrate hand and nail care. Girls could begin a program and monitor their success.

9. Include in some of your lessons recordings that will enhance the topic of those chapters. Examples include some such as: Billy Joel's "Eye of the Storm" video and/or recording "Stormfront" and watermen of Long Island Sound song" The Downeaster Alexa" or Bruce Hornsby's tale of woe of the Chesapeake watermen, "The Tide Will Rise" from *Harbor Lights.* Play a recording of " I Wonder As I Wander" by Barbara Streisand, etc. or have an able musical student perform and explain its difficulty. Students respond well to the use of music.(Is this school?)

10. Write to Katherine Paterson asking her questions students have composed. You could send a class set of letters in one large envelope.

11. Practice ordering out of a Sears (or some other store's)mail order catalog. Try to imagine what it would be like not to be able to go the mall and shop like most of them probably do.

More Activities - *Jacob Have I Loved* page 2

12. Research music, fashions, hairstyles, etc. of this era. Have a mock victory celebration day with music, costumes, posters, etc.

13. Show Reader's Digest's set of videos (or some other) on the Homefront Years.

14. Invite a willing relative of your students in to share information about this time period, both from the homefront and overseas.

15. Have students interview someone who lived during this time period, preferably a relative. Have students compose questions together for their interviews. They could then make a booklet with the information in it for display. Have them illustrate the cover with something they learned about the times from their interview.

16. Allow students to select a character from the novel. Have them dress like them, speak like them; assume their persona. Create a talk show format with these characters as the guests. Have a student volunteer to be the host. Others not involved will be the audience, questioning the characters. One of your students could pretend to be a trained psychologist who comes out later in the show to help the panel solve their problems. Have a topic like: sibling rivalry, living with your extended family, i.e. problems encountered in the novel. Allow the class to decide as much as possible. Have questions from the audience ready prior to the show day. You could have students try out for the parts. Remind them to keep it on the up and up, not to mimic some of the seedier talk shows. This will require students to take an in-depth look into characterization in the novel.

17. View a filmstrip on Katherine Paterson.

18. If at all feasible, take the class crabbing or oystering or invite a waterman to your class to share. Discuss the differences between commercial seafood gatherers and recreational . This could be tied in with the project and the following question.

19. Research the problems watermen face today to gain understanding of why this has fast become a dying tradition.

20. Compare life on an isolated island with your students's lives. Have them come up with a list of major differences, advantages, disadvantages, etc. Perhaps they could illustrate differences and display.

21. Make a study of storms to hit the East coast in the 1940's. Are the ones in the novel authentic?

22. View a film on the Chesapeake Bay.

More Activities - *Jacob Have I Loved* page 3

23. Students who like board games may want to create one using information from this novel. Some students could work together as a group to complete this task. Encourage them to look at setting to illustrate their board and possibly use vocabulary, characters, plot, etc. for question cards.

24. Have students bring in samples of contests from magazines similar to the one Wheeze entered from LYRICS UNLIMITED. Discuss the odds of actually winning something like that. Students could enter a few and see what type of response they receive. Compare them to the mimeographed answer Wheeze received

25. Have students read the following newspaper article and discuss. How does this situation reflect current society values? In what ways can they compare Smith Island to Rass? How would they feel if they had to do this? How would Caroline and Wheeze have felt? They could write letters to the children.

WORD SEARCH - Jacob Have I Loved

```
B T R I C E C U L L I N G T M M B S H J
U R L B R W M S P O X C H O I O A K I K
S U A O I O S A H Q U G N N D U L I T T
T I D H S N U K I A I I E G W N T P L S
E T I E F D S F R N N E S S I T I J E Y
R T E M I E A N A W L T R E F A M A R W
M J S E E R N U M G H A Y U E I O C H X
S E Z N L W A S R J E E N Q H N R K U Z
H R T M D S A A W S O L E D H S E D R J
A G T H E X S T Y G I S Y Z S J K R R J
D E Q C O S P D E M N L E M E U O E I Q
O N L M Y D U M I R L V A P X I P D C V
W S E D S R I T Y A M L D Y H L J G A L
T F G G T T E S C D L E K K W L M E N T
N E A U E D P B M E M P N C P I S S E T
K R C N R X I R K H A E R U P A A W G C
X R Y N U S A A B C R Q T A R B J S N
H Y G Y W X N D D R Y B T N C D B P W H
F K T S N B O S R F L O S E I R A S N G
D N L A O D M H R A A D D K F R T O G C
R A V C A P T A I N N Y M M I J H O R T
D E A K H X S W S T D K M S C F R K Z L
R J A C P S G U T T D L R A E P F K M K
```

BALTIMORE	GUNNYSACK	LADIES	PEABODY	SKIPJACK
BOHEME	GUT	LEGACY	PEARL	SOOK
BRADSHAW	HIRAM	LOUISE	PIANO	SPCA
BUSTER	HITLER	MAINLAND	POKER	SUN
CALL	HURRICANE	MARYLAND	PROG	SUSAN
CAPTAIN	JACOB	MAST	RANK	TIME
CRISFIELD	JEAN	METHODISM	RASS	TONGS
CULLING	JERGENS	MIDWIFE	RICE	TRUDY
DREDGES	JIMMY	MOUNTAINS	SABBATH	TRUITT
EELGRASS	JOSEPH	NIGHT	SEARS	UNLIMITED
ESAU	JUILLIARD	OYSTER	SHADOW	WATERMEN
FDR	KELLAMS	PACIFIC	SHANTY	WHEEZE
FERRY	KENTUCKY	PARIS	SKIFF	WONDER

WORD SEARCH ANSWER KEY - Jacob Have I Loved

```
B T R I C E C U L L I N G T M M B S H
U R L B R W M S O H O I O A K I
S U A O I O S A H U G N D U L I T
T I D H S N U I A I E G W N T P L
E T I F D S R N N E S S I T J E
R T E M I E A A W L T R E F A M A R
M J S E R U M G H A Y U E I O C H
S E L W A R J E E N N R K U
H T T D S A A S O L E D S J K R R
A G H E S T Y I S Z S J K R I
D E O S D E M L E M E U O E I
O N L Y D U M I R L A P I P D C
W S S R I T A M L Y H L G A
F G G T T E S C L E K L E N
E A U E D P B M E M P N C I S S E
R C N R I R K A E U P A A
R Y N U S A A R A T A R B
Y Y N D Y B N C D B P
F S B O S R L O S E I A S
D N A O M H R A A D K F R T O G
R A C A P T A I N Y M M I J H O
E K S W S D K S C F R K
J A C P S G U T T L R A E P F
```

BALTIMORE	GUNNYSACK	LADIES	PEABODY	SKIPJACK
BOHEME	GUT	LEGACY	PEARL	SOOK
BRADSHAW	HIRAM	LOUISE	PIANO	SPCA
BUSTER	HITLER	MAINLAND	POKER	SUN
CALL	HURRICANE	MARYLAND	PROG	SUSAN
CAPTAIN	JACOB	MAST	RANK	TIME
CRISFIELD	JEAN	METHODISM	RASS	TONGS
CULLING	JERGENS	MIDWIFE	RICE	TRUDY
DREDGES	JIMMY	MOUNTAINS	SABBATH	TRUITT
EELGRASS	JOSEPH	NIGHT	SEARS	UNLIMITED
ESAU	JUILLIARD	OYSTER	SHADOW	WATERMEN
FDR	KELLAMS	PACIFIC	SHANTY	WHEEZE
FERRY	KENTUCKY	PARIS	SKIFF	WONDER

CROSSWORD - *Jacob Have I Loved*

CROSSWORD CLUES *Jacob Have I Loved*

ACROSS

1. Inland Maryland town
4. Named for Shakespearian lady and Susan (2 words)
7. Used by the Captain to view Call and Wheeze
11. Narrow channel of water
12. Swindled out of birthright by Biblical twin
13. Wheeze's crabbing boat
15. Chesapeake island near Crisfield
17. Graduated a nurse-midwife from Rass
19. Hearing organ
20. Woman Hiram marries
21. McCall Purnell
23. King of the jungle
24. Source of Wheeze's jokes
26. ___ curtains; Darkened window coverings
29. 32nd president
31. Man's title
33. To fish for crab
34. Fuel for scriptural quote by Grandma
35. Store where islanders order shoes
36. Baltimore newspaper Wheeze reads
37. Wheeze beats Caroline satisfactorily
38. Woman's apparel

DOWN

2. ___ Unlimited; Misspelled Wheeze's name
3. Came to Rass to teach
5. Waterman father of twins
6. Lady crab
7. Naval base in Hawaii bombed by Japanese (2 words)
8. Island streets; ___ shell
9. Marine plant with ribbon-like leaves
10. A blue crab ready to shed its shell (2 words)
14. Only island transportation
16. Where Wheeze wants to take cats
18. Spies on another spy
20. Fork-like device used to retrieve oysters
22. New York City music conservatory
25. Island religion
27. Focal point of Mr. Rice's music program
28. Continental part of state
30. Large frames with nets used to collect shellfish
32. Place Susan wanted to go to write poetry
33. Instrument owned only by Bradshaws on island

CROSSWORD ANSWER KEY - *Jacob Have I Loved*

	S	A	L	I	S	B	U	R	Y		P	O	R	T	I	A		S	U	E	
			Y		U								R			O					
P	E	R	I	S	C	O	P	E		R		G	U	T		O					
E		I		A		Y		E	S	A	U		I			S	K	I	F	F	
A		V		N		S		L		N			T							E	
R	A	S	S			T		G		K	E	N	T	U	C	K	Y			R	
L			P			E	A	R		P						O				R	
H			C			R		A		E			T	R	U	D	Y			Y	
A		C	A	L	L			S		E			O			N					
R						J		S		L	I	O	N			T	I	M	E		
B	L	A	C	K	O	U	T			E			G			E		E		M	
O		A				I		F	D	R			S	I	R			T		A	
R		R				L		R		P					S			H		I	
	P	R	O	G		L		L	E	G	A	C	Y		P			O		N	
	I		L			I		D		R			Y		D			D		L	
	A		I			A		G		I					I			I		A	
	N		N			R		E		S	E	A	R	S				S	U	N	
P	O	K	E	R		D	R	E	S	S								M		D	

154

MATCHING QUIZ/WORKSHEET 1 - *Jacob Have I Loved*

___ 1. Wheeze   A. Baltimore music school
___ 2. Culling   B. Named for Shakespearian lady and Susan
___ 3. Midwife   C. Male blue crab
___ 4. Skipjack   D. Sara Louise's nickname
___ 5. Captain   E. Delivers babies
___ 6. Rank Peeler   F. Has a fiance in Baltimore
___ 7. Peabody   G. Crab ready to shed its shell
___ 8. Joseph   H. Sorting shellfish by size
___ 9. Jimmy   I. Large Maryland seaport
___10. Waterman   J. Earned title of watermen fifty or older
___11. La Boheme   K. Waterman's vessel
___12. Salisbury   L. Smiled like a man who would sing to oysters
___13. Mr. Rice   M. Follows the water
___14. Jergens   N. Debuts Caroline as Musetta in New Haven
___15. Eelgrass   O. Gets thrown against the wall
___16. Paterson   P. Inland Maryland town
___17. Baltimore   Q. Ribbon-like leaved plant
___18. The Shadow   R. Knows what evil lurks in the hearts of men
___19. Methodism   S. Island religion
___20. Portia Sue   T. Author of novel

KEY: MATCHING QUIZ/WORKSHEET 1 - *Jacob Have I Loved*

__D__ 1. Wheeze
__H__ 2. Culling
__E__ 3. Midwife
__K__ 4. Skipjack
__J__ 5. Captain
__G__ 6. Rank Peeler
__A__ 7. Peabody
__L__ 8. Joseph
__C__ 9. Jimmy
__M__ 10. Waterman
__N__ 11. La Boheme
__P__ 12. Salisbury
__F__ 13. Mr. Rice
__O__ 14. Jergens
__R__ 15. Eelgrass
__T__ 16. Paterson
__I__ 17. Baltimore
__Q__ 18. The Shadow
__S__ 19. Methodism
__B__ 20. Portia Sue

A. Baltimore music school
B. Named for Shakespearian lady and Susan
C. Male blue crab
D. Sara Louise's nickname
E. Delivers babies
F. Has a fiance in Baltimore
G. Crab ready to shed its shell
H. Sorting shellfish by size
I. Large Maryland seaport
J. Earned title of watermen fifty or older
K. Waterman's vessel
L. Smiled like a man who would sing to oysters
M. Follows the water
N. Debuts Caroline as Musetta in New Haven
O. Gets thrown against the wall
P. Inland Maryland town
Q. Knows what evil lurks in the hearts of men
R. Ribbon-like leaved plant
S. Island religion
T. Author of novel

MATCHING QUIZ/WORKSHEET 2 - *Jacob Have I Loved*

___ 1. Ferry   A. To fish for crab

___ 2. Esau   B. Used by Captain to view Call and Wheeze

___ 3. Prog   C. Darkened window coverings

___ 4. Gut   D. Mountain-locked Appalachian valley

___ 5. Sun   E. Only island transportation

___ 6. Crisfield   F. Where Wheeze wants to take cats

___ 7. O Holy Night   G. Swindled out of birthright by Biblical twin

___ 8. Periscope   H. Narrow channel of water

___ 9. Poker   I. New York City music school

___10. Mast   J. Female blue crab

___11. Sook   K. Maryland town closest to Rass by ferry

___12. SPCA   L. Sung by Betty Jean Boyd at Christmas program

___13. Blackout curtains   M. Three island boys aboard same ship died there

___14. Pearl Harbor   N. Wheeze beats Caroline satisfactorily

___15. Hiram   O. Felled by Hiram during storm

___16. Lyrics Unlimited   P. Island streets

___17. Truitt   Q. Island native who returns after fifty years

___18. Juilliard   R. Baltimore newspaper Wheeze read

___19. Oyster shell   S. Naval base in Hawaii bombed by Japanese

___20. South Pacific   T. Misspelled Wheeze's name on letter

KEY: MATCHING QUIZ/WORKSHEET 2 - *Jacob Have I Loved*

E 1. Ferry		A. To fish for crab
G 2. Esau		B. Used by Captain to view Call and Wheeze
A 3. Prog		C. Darkened window coverings
H 4. Gut		D. Mountain-locked Appalachian valley
R 5. Sun		E. Only island transportation
K 6. Crisfield		F. Where Wheeze wants to take cats
L 7. O Holy Night		G. Swindled out of birthright by Biblical twin
B 8. Periscope		H. Narrow channel of water
N 9. Poker		I. New York City music school
O 10. Mast		J. Female blue crab
J 11. Sook		K. Maryland town closest to Rass by ferry
F 12. SPCA		L. Sung by Betty Jean Boyd at Christmas program
C 13. Blackout curtains		M. Three island boys aboard same ship died there
S 14. Pearl Harbor		N. Wheeze beats Caroline satisfactorily
Q 15. Hiram		O. Felled by Hiram during storm
T 16. Lyrics Unlimited		P. Island streets
D 17. Truitt		Q. Island native who returns after fifty years
I 18. Juilliard		R. Baltimore newspaper Wheeze read
P 19. Oyster shell		S. Naval base in Hawaii bombed by Japanese
M 20. South Pacific		T. Misspelled Wheeze's name on letter

JUGGLE LETTER REVIEW GAME CLUE SHEET - *Jacob Have I Loved*

SCRAMBLED	WORD	CLUE
AROLEBRARPH	PEARL HARBOR	Naval Base in Hawaii bombed by Japanese
AMSLELK	KELLAMS	General store and post office on Rass
CASP	SPCA	Where Wheeze wants to take cats
AANLNMDI	MAINLAND	Continental part of state
NAYMRDLA	MARYLAND	University Wheeze attends first
RIANCOEL	CAROLINE	Focal point of Mr. Rice's music program
URITTT	TRUITT	Mountain-locked Appalachian valley
PNEERKERAL	RANKPEELER	Crab ready to shed its shell
OITUNSMAN	MOUNTAINS	Wheeze longs to see
MEHEOLAB	LABOHEME	Debuts Caroline as Musetta in New Haven
TNEATYBJE	BETTYJEAN	Sings "O Holy Night " at Christmas program
SSNUA	SUSAN	Came to Rass to teach school
FEDIIWM	MIDWIFE	Delivers babies
SPOJHE	JOSEPH	Smiled like a man who would sing to the oysters
APISR	PARIS	Where Susan wanted to write poetry
GPRO	PROG	Fish for crab
ANEURHRCI	HURRICANE	Reduced island's cat population by two-thirds
SIIELDFRC	CRISFIELD	Maryland town closest to island by ferry
EEHZEW	WHEEZE	Sara Louise's nickname
EONRAOBGM	BOOMERANG	Came back every time the Australian threw it away
URTY	TRUDY	Woman Hiram marries
KSFIF	SKIFF	Wheeze's crabbing boat
TABASHB	SABBATH	Holy Day
DBAEYPO	PEABODY	Baltimore music school
OGCRPRIAE	PAREGORIC	Household remedy
ERDDSGE	DREDGES	Large frames with nets used to collect shellfish
YBSSIARUL	SALISBURY	Inland Maryland town
NUKKETYC	KENTUCKY	Graduates a nurse-midwife from Rass
AAPNTIC	CAPTAIN	Earned title of fifty year old waterman
ONPTRASE	PATERSON	Author of novel
GCILULN	CULLING	Sorting shellfish by size
SIOULE	LOUISE	Cranky Grandma Bradshaw

VOCABULARY RESOURCE MATERIALS

VOCABULARY WORD SEARCH - Jacob Have I Loved

```
B L M A C H I N A T I O N S F C L W H X
E U P R E T E N T I O U S C B V Q X N D
N G S C R E F U R B I S H E D P K B X F
E U A F O W D P T N E R R O T A N H G G
V B B J T N I N V S X L D M L R Q B D N
O R O Q N T T X D H U G B E Z A N E O X
L I T D E G M E V R L D C L N G L L M D
E O E O V R D V M A T S Z K S O C K I Q
N U U X R S O F Z P A S H N J R H C N Y
T S R P E T U L A N T Y N A T I L A O R
L L K Q F T S D X E I L C R R C S H U W
Y Y Q C I C E G R L O R S L L D P S S W
A C D L B L S R N I N E I X H Q S M E R
O B E I L T A D X R L G Q V S D U A X M
B E E E L P G E F O Y N F A U E O R A R
L F F R I A L H X N R I J U O L R M S Q
I U N N R L P S M Y I G Z D I E E L P Y
G D C K Q A H I F I C K L E R G H T E C
I D G L F X T N D Y I J R V A A C J R K
N L R J S D V I R A S W C I C T A H A N
G E B R C R C M O V T K P L E I E S T D
G D D E L U S I O N S E X L R O R G E B
N D E T N U A D N U S R D E P N T H D G
```

ABERRATIONS	DOUSE	LITANY	PRECARIOUS	TERRAPIN
BEFUDDLED	EXASPERATED	LUGUBRIOUSLY	PRETENTIOUS	TORRENT
BENEVOLENTLY	EXULTATION	LYRICIST	RAMSHACKLE	TREACHEROUS
CAJOLED	FELLED	MACHINATIONS	RANKLE	UNDAUNTED
CONTEMPT	FERVENT	OBLIGING	REFURBISHED	VAUDEVILLE
DELEGATION	FICKLE	OMINOUS	RIVULET	
DELUSIONS	FUTILE	PARAGORIC	SABOTEUR	
DILAPIDATED	GINGERLY	PETULANT	SHARDS	
DIMINISHED	IRONY	PITEOUS	SHRAPNEL	

VOCABULARY WORD SEARCH ANSWER KEY - Jacob Have I Loved

ABERRATIONS	DOUSE	LITANY	PRECARIOUS	TERRAPIN
BEFUDDLED	EXASPERATED	LUGUBRIOUSLY	PRETENTIOUS	TORRENT
BENEVOLENTLY	EXULTATION	LYRICIST	RAMSHACKLE	TREACHEROUS
CAJOLED	FELLED	MACHINATIONS	RANKLE	UNDAUNTED
CONTEMPT	FERVENT	OBLIGING	REFURBISHED	VAUDEVILLE
DELEGATION	FICKLE	OMINOUS	RIVULET	
DELUSIONS	FUTILE	PARAGORIC	SABOTEUR	
DILAPIDATED	GINGERLY	PETULANT	SHARDS	
DIMINISHED	IRONY	PITEOUS	SHRAPNEL	

VOCABULARY CROSSWORD - *Jacob Have I Loved*

VOCABULARY CROSSWORD CLUES *Jacob Have I Loved*

ACROSS
1. Frustrated
6. Mock or jeer
9. Flood; overflow
10. Hopeless
11. Song writer
13. Swindled out of birthright by Biblical twin
15. Belonging to him
16. Not discouraged or disheartened
18. Black, sticky substance; ___ and feather
19. Woman Hiram marries
21. 32nd president
23. Inheritance; sum of money
24. Baltimore newspaper Wheeze reads
25. Came to Rass to teach
26. Lady crab
27. Ingested food
28. Source of Wheeze's jokes
30. Head cover
32. Fragments of a brittle substance, as of glass or metal
33. Crab shack
34. To fish for crab
35. Focal point of Mr. Rice's music program
36. Island streets; ___ shell

DOWN
2. Contrast; incongruity
3. Plural of man
4. Hard to pin down; slippery
5. Made smaller; lessened
6. North American aquatic turtle
7. Never changing; strict
8. Extremely unsafe
11. Mournfully; gloomily
12. Small talk
14. Irritable or ill-tempered; peevish
17. False beliefs or opinions
20. I ___ As I Wander; Caroline's Christmas program solo
22. Chesapeake island near Crisfield
25. Knows what evil lurks in the hearts of men
28. Fork-like device used to retrieve oysters
29. McCall Purnell
31. Question

VOCABULARY CROSSWORD ANSWER KEY - *Jacob Have I Loved*

VOCABULARY WORKSHEET 1 - *Jacob Have I Loved*

____ 1. Unrelenting   A. Puzzled; perplexed

____ 2. Torrent   B. Small talk

____ 3. Reverie   C. Removed

____ 4. Taunt   D. Defiant; wild

____ 5. Rivulet   E. Showing great emotion; ardent

____ 6. Obliging   F. Akwardness

____ 7. Petulant   G. Helpful

____ 8. Fervent   H. Routinely; impersonally

____ 9. Discomposure   I. Irritable or ill-tempered; peevish

____ 10. Extricated   J. Puffed-up; self-important

____ 11. Inanities   K. Flood; overflow

____ 12. Contemptuous   L. Never changing; rigid

____ 13. Perfunctorily   M. Dream

____ 14. Befuddled   N. Refinished

____ 15. Pretentious   O. Meager existence

____ 16. Subsistence   P. Rightness

____ 17. Refurbished   Q. Examination; close attention

____ 18. Propriety   R. One who sabotages

____ 19. Saboteur   S. Mock or jeer

____ 20. Scrutiny   T. Small stream

KEY: VOCABULARY WORKSHEET 1 - *Jacob Have I Loved*

L	1. Unrelenting	A. Puzzled; perplexed
K	2. Torrent	B. Small talk
M	3. Reverie	C. Removed
S	4. Taunt	D. Defiant; wild
T	5. Rivulet	E. Showing great emotion; ardent
G	6. Obliging	F. Akwardness
I	7. Petulant	G. Helpful
E	8. Fervent	H. Routinely; impersonally
F	9. Discomposure	I. Irritable or ill-tempered; peevish
C	10. Extricated	J. Puffed-up; self-important
B	11. Inanities	K. Flood; overflow
D	12. Contemptuous	L. Never changing; rigid
H	13. Perfunctorily	M. Dream
A	14. Befuddled	N. Refinished
J	15. Pretentious	O. Meager existence
O	16. Subsistence	P. Rightness
N	17. Refurbished	Q. Examination; close attention
P	18. Propriety	R. One who sabotages
R	19. Saboteur	S. Mock or jeer
Q	20. Scrutiny	T. Small stream

VOCABULARY WORKSHEET 2 - *Jacob Have I Loved*

____ 1. Vaudeville   A. Irritate or cause resentment

____ 2. Treacherous   B. Objection; protest

____ 3. Savagery   C. Abandonment; denial

____ 4. Renunciation   D. Stage act

____ 5. Remonstrance   E. Extremely unsafe

____ 6. Rankle   F. Cruelty

____ 7. Adamant   G. Immovable; rigid

____ 8. Benevolently   H. Kindly

____ 9. Contentious   I. Quarrelsome

____ 10. Deprivation   J. Loss

____ 11. Paregoric   K. Shabby; neglected

____ 12. Mortal   L. Made smaller; lessened

____ 13. Lugubriously   M. Put out; extinguish

____ 14. Litany   N. Angered or annoyed greatly

____ 15. Gingerly   O. Changeable

____ 16. Fickle   P. Carefully

____ 17. Exasperated   Q. Mournfully, gloomily

____ 18. Douse   R. Fatal; deadly

____ 19. Diminished   S. Opium medicine

____ 20. Dilapidated   T. Series of prayers

KEY: VOCABULARY WORKSHEET 2 - *Jacob Have I Loved*

D	1. Vaudeville	A.	Irritate or cause resentment
E	2. Treacherous	B.	Objection; protest
F	3. Savagery	C.	Abandonment; denial
C	4. Renunciation	D.	Stage act
B	5. Remonstrance	E.	Extremely unsafe
A	6. Rankle	F.	Cruelty
G	7. Adamant	G.	Immovable; rigid
H	8. Benevolently	H.	Kindly
I	9. Contentious	I.	Quarrelsome
J	10. Deprivation	J.	Loss
S	11. Paregoric	K.	Shabby; neglected
R	12. Mortal	L.	Made smaller; lessened
Q	13. Lugubriously	M.	Put out; extinguish
T	14. Litany	N.	Angered or annoyed greatly
P	15. Gingerly	O.	Changeable
O	16. Fickle	P.	Carefully
N	17. Exasperated	Q.	Mournfully, gloomily
M	18. Douse	R.	Fatal; deadly
L	19. Diminished	S.	Opium medicine
K	20. Dilapidated	T.	Series of prayers

VOCABULARY JUGGLE LETTER REVIEW GAME CLUES - *Jacob Have I Loved*

SCRAMBLED	WORD	CLUE
NBRAASOETRI	ABERRATIONS	Quirks, abnormalities
SUEEVLI	ELUSIVE	Hard to pin down; slippery
UOSDE	DOUSE	Put out; extinguish
RLAMOT	MORTAL	Fatal; deadly
OYRNI	IRONY	Contrast; incongruity
TSUPIEO	PITEOUS	Pitiful; pathetic
CGELAY	LEGACY	Inheritance; sum of money
GIVINCNON	CONNIVING	Scheming
TTEESNPOURI	PRETENTIOUS	Puffed-up; self-important
NIATYL	LITANY	Series of prayers
CRRNAO	RANCOR	Bitter resentment
EIRTARNP	TERRAPIN	North American aquatic turtle
YTCILISR	LYRICIST	Song writer
DHSRAS	SHARDS	Brittle fragments; glass
NUATT	TAUNT	Mock or jeer
SSMAACR	SARCASM	Remark meant to wound
KELCFI	FICKLE	Changable
CIDIYO	IDIOCY	Extreme foolishness
HISINIMDED	DIMINISHED	Made smaller; lessened
EEFLLDE	FELLED	Chopped
AHHEENT	HEATHEN	Unbeliever; pagan
LNDGSEEAOIN	DELEGATIONS	Assigned group
LURITA	RITUAL	Custom
EAKNKR	RANKLE	Irritate or cause resentment
RYLGGIEN	GINGERLY	Carefully
EORETNR	TORRENT	Flood; overflow
SAUOCCRPII	CAPRICIOUS	Erratic; unpredictable
OONMISU	OMINOUS	Threatening
EEDDDFBUL	BEFUDDLED	Puzzled; perplexed
RGQEAAUDLN	QUADRANGLE	Courtyard enclosed by buildings
LLNMEAYOHC	MELANCHOLY	Sadness
LUFETI	FUTILE	Hopeless
EEEVRRI	REVERIE	Dream
TTTEESDIU	DESTITUTE	Very poor
NNDDUUTNA	UNDAUNTED	Not discouraged or disheartened

www.ingramcontent.com/pod-product-compliance
Lightning Source LLC
LaVergne TN
LVHW081534060526
838200LV00048B/2082